To Elizabeth,
'HAPPY CHRISTMAS'
love Sarah

YOUR INNER SECRETS EXPOSED

YOUR INNER SECRETS EXPOSED

by

G_____T OAKLEY

W. Foulsham & Co. Ltd.

London · New York · Toronto · Cape Town · Sydney

W. Foulsham & Company Limited
Yeovil Road, Slough, Berkshire, SL1 4JH

ISBN 0-572-01334-5

Printed in Great Britain by
St Edmundsbury Press, Bury St Edmunds, Suffolk.

CONTENTS

INTRODUCTION 9

HOW TO USE THIS GUIDE 13

PART ONE 17

Your Psycho-Signs
Individual Psychological Guidance
from the Twelve Sun Signs

1. Weak Characteristics
2. Strong Characteristics
3. Dominant Ambitions
4. Chief Capabilities
5. Pet Phobia
6. Best Course of Action in Life
7. Possible Peak-Age of Power
8. Your Psycho-Type

The Stars Pass from Mental to Physical 51

PART TWO 53

Your Zodiacure
Individual Health Guidance from the
Twelve Signs of the Zodiac

1. Constitution
2. Deficiency Mineral
3. Essential Vitamin-Needs
4. Special Diet
5. Breathing Exercises
6. Possible Peak-Age of Virility, Physical Perfection

The Stars Pass on to Your Personal 'Aura' 77

PART THREE 79

Your Star-Aura
Individual Guidance to Your Positive and Negative
'drives' and influences, your love-life and emotional
outlets

1. Your Sense of Humour
2. Your Positive 'Success Drive'
3. Your Negative 'Pull-Back'
4. Your Love Life

The Stars Pass on to Your Personal 'Make-Up' 93

PART FOUR 97

Your Personal Star 'Make-Up'

Individual Indications of Facial, Physical appearance, Physical Weaknesses to strengthen, Hints on Your Dress Sense

1. Dominant Facial Characteristics
2. Dominant Physical Characteristics
3. Look After Your . . .
4. Your Dress Sense

    Career Indications for the Twelve Sun Signs   110

Present and Future Moves for more Success at your Job   120

    Bureau of Careers   123

    The Stars turn to the Material Things   125

PART FIVE 127

Your Star Sign

Showing Your Metal, Stone, Colours, Numbers, Days, Future Finances and who best to Mix with or Marry

1. Individual Metal
2. Sympathetic Stone
3. Harmonious Colours
4. Sympathetic Herb
5. Lucky Number
6. Lucky Day
7. Health and Your Number
8. Future Finances
9. Mix with or Marry . . .

    Specimen Astrological Summary-Sheet   140

SUMMING-UP 141

The Stars Pass into Orbit and leave you to your Future Hopes

The meaning of Astrology. The Star's Influences on the Time you were Born. Your Positive Planning Months. Your Month to Marry. Parents' Guide to their Children's Marriage Hopes. Parents' Guide to their Children's Career Hopes.

INTRODUCTION

A good use to which a study of the Stars can be put is not only to hope to predict the future—but to know how to base *future moves for success* upon the dominant characteristics you possess from the Sun Sign under which you were born.

There are twelve signs of the Zodiac—one for each month of the year. Each sign is the name of the star which wields certain mysterious influences over you. Born under such-and-such a star—you are pre-disposed to certain actions, have certain characteristics that make you different from a person born under another star's influence.

Using knowledge of the stars to the best advantage embraces study of the dominant characteristics, psychological aberrations and quirks, health tendencies and personality-traits possessed by you as a direct result of your birth date and the star which was in the ascendency when you were born.

A horoscope is a very intricate reading of a star's influences. This book sums up the psychological influences, the constitutional influences, the personality-drives and the individual make-up of persons born under each of the twelve signs of the Zodiac.

The information contained in this book can help you to cast your own and your friends' horoscope. Can help you to guide members of your family, decide what investments to make, how to fashion your child's career. A horoscope consists of a circular 'chart' of your life. The pages of this book will give you a complete picture of the sort of person you are, the sort of people you have to deal with, make friends with, live with—or marry.

If you can first learn to understand yourself, find out what sort of a person you are, what elements of your make-up can make or mar your life, what precautions should be taken to keep your health up to standard—how to direct your impulses and control your personality—you will understand what life *could* have in store for you.

You will also be able to help those around you to control and to direct *their* lives.

Many people, in an attempt to begin to understand themselves, have no jumping-off point. That is not the case with *you*. You now have a guide that begins with the first and most important stage of individual development—the day you were *born*.

This book takes you through your emotional development, your physical growth and finalises the picture of *you* with those elements that, if properly used, can help you through life in a manner that, though not necessarily placid, at least will be as successful as your stars—and your commonsense—will allow it to be.

Do not look for *predictions* in the accepted sense of the word. Look for *tendencies*. Pre-dispositions. Likelihoods. Portents. Hopes. All these will be based on common characteristics possessed by and displayed by you (and your friends) according to the traditional and accepted influences of the stars.

Upon portents and pre-dispositions can life be shaped and moulded. Upon knowledge of what the stars have done for you, what gifts (and disadvantages) they have bestowed upon you, you can plan your present and future moves, understand why the past has, perhaps, brought its failures. You can learn what moves to make *now* that will make your future more positive. You can learn to strengthen all your little weaknesses. Resolve to turn past mistakes into constructive patterns for the future.

Learn, also, why certain people have been bad for you. Why friendships have fallen by the wayside—once promising associations turned on you.

Sceptics dismiss the influence of the stars with a shrug. Yet, the Universe was there in the very beginning of life. From the great Beyond we draw many scientific facts that help the world go round. As the moon exerts influence on the tides—so do the stars exert influences on individuals.

Those who choose to believe, do so in a cool, calm, reasoned fashion. They acknowledge the existence of a Deity who put the stars in the heavens in the first place. They find peace of mind in the knowledge these heavenly bodies are there for the purpose of assisting the Greater Power to direct and to control *individual* destiny—so that every man, woman and child can have a place on earth in which to *find fulfilment*.

There are no confusing technicalities in this book which belong, strictly, to the Astrologer and Mystic. Here is a study of the Stars you can apply to yourself, your friends and your dear ones. Psychological aspects, individual characteristics, health indications, personality development—are all here.

Your taste in dress, the quality of your sense of humour complete the picture of you and your associates. For the health-conscious, there are vitamin needs, mineral-deficiency indications and breathing exercises.

This all-the-year-round guide shows you how best to tackle the future, make the most of the present and compensate for mistakes made in the past.

Gilbert Oakley

HOW TO USE THIS GUIDE

For your own guidance—

ONE. Study the Psycho-Signs, according to your date of birth as it falls between the two dates shown for each Sun Sign. Note your weak points, make the most of your strong points. Sort out your chief capabilities, pair them off with your dominant ambitions and see how best you are making the *most* of them. Get to understand your 'pet phobia' and do your best to *fight it*. Learn your best course of action in life and note your possible peak age of power.

TWO. Study your constitution in the Zodiacure. Try a month's course on the health diets, do all the breathing exercises. Carry out these routines from time to time throughout the year. Make up your deficiency mineral, and fill your vitamin needs by eating the right foods, by taking biochemic salts. Note your possible peak age of virility and do not try to overdo things after that age has been reached.

THREE. Develop your personality through the Star-Aura. Assess your sense of humour. Examine your present life and locate the dominant 'negative pull-back' that prevents your going *forward*. Where your sex-drive is concerned, apply this to your married or unmarried state as it obtains at the moment. From what you learn of your money sense, re-adjust personal financial matters. Where creative abilities are shown, try to make the most of them, either as a hobby or as a serious vocation.

FOUR. Project your personality-pattern by learning what your Star Make-Up has to show. Decide to what facial and physical type you belong. Make careful note of your social and business assets. Try to reconcile them to your ability to make friends. Carefully study your emotional outlook. The way you look at life is of paramount importance. It determines how others will look at *you*.

FIVE. Your Star-Sign, in the last part of the guide, will show your metal, stone, colour. See you always carry something that contains the lucky elements indicated. Make a note of your lucky days and months for making investments, buying and selling, trying to improve your career-hopes. Concentrate all your energies to pursuing your dearest desires *on* those days and months. Choose or change your friends according to *their* Sun Signs as shown. Finally—base future moves on *all* information and guidance you will have received in this guide, paying particular attention to your career-indications and to those of your children—for the future.

For your Friends and Members of your Family—
Get their birth dates between the two dates shown for each Sun Sign. Advise them on all mental and physical points shown in each of the sections. Advise them as to their lucky numbers, etc., by using a copy of the Astrological Summary.

NOTE. This guide is to be used for an indefinite period. It does not forecast only for a day, a week, a month or a year. It gives an overall picture of potential for your life from the moment you learn and absorb what it has to teach. It also does the same for your friends and for those who belong to you.

YOUR PSYCHO-SIGNS cover your *mental attitude*.

YOUR ZODIACURE covers your *health trends*.

YOUR STAR-AURA tells you the *sort of person you are*.

YOUR STAR MAKE-UP shows you *how you should look*.

YOUR STAR-SIGN tells you of the *material things you should always carry, the best days to do certain things, how to shape your future based on today*.

YOUR CAREER-INDICATIONS show the jobs in life in which you could excel. Show how you can improve on present working conditions.

PARENTS' GUIDE TO THEIR CHILDREN'S FUTURE CAREER-HOPES helps parents in choosing careers for their children, tells them what to expect—and how not to expect too much.

PART ONE

Your Psycho-Signs

*Individual Psychological Guidance from the
Twelve Sun Signs*

The Sun Signs commence with December in each Part, to
make a full year's reading, and not with the First Sign of the
Zodiac which is lined up with March to April—*Aries*.

10th House

10th Sign of the Zodiac

CAPRICORN

SATURN
Ruling Planet

December 23—January 20

WEAK CHARACTER POINTS

You are apt to underrate yourself and lose good opportunities for advancement. A moody nature makes you misunderstood by many. If in trouble of any sort, you magnify the situation until it becomes larger than life. This way—you make mountains out of very small molehills. Your life has, so far, been an up-and-down affair. That is largely your own doing. Try to see things in their right perspective from now on. You will find things are never as bad as you think they are. And other people will not be deluded into thinking you are really in trouble when, in fact, you are not. You are the sort of person who should spend a lot of time each day willing yourself forward—giving yourself little pep-talks from time to time. You would find this would work wonders for you in time.

STRONG CHARACTER POINTS

You are a deep thinker. Possibly a little too deep, for this gets you involved, from time to time, in things that would better be avoided. However, do not be discouraged. The deep thinker usually makes something of his thoughts. It is possible you will, one day, evolve something that might well take you a long way up the ladder to success. Hard working, you follow-through to the bitter end. This may be a bit tiring from time to time, so give yourself plenty of rest and relaxation when opportunity offers. You like doing things for others. This makes you well liked and is a good thing in your favour. Where organising is concerned, others will look to you to make a good job of most everything. Where friends are concerned, you are extremely loyal—perhaps a little too much so. This may make certain sly people take advantage

19

of you. Try tempering loyalty with a little more discrimination. You will pretty soon find who are your real friends. Music appeals. All sorts. This is good for it enables you to enjoy yourself in mixed company and to be able to discuss the old and the new with a great show of intelligence and musical appreciation. A certain sort of magnetism in your nature draws others to you. Make the most of this highly desirable quality. Not all possess it.

DOMINANT AMBITIONS

To teach—or to lead others. To stand on a platform and speak. To be head of something really worthwhile but not necessarily as your job in life. Socially, maybe. With your magnetic personality—you could well hold an audience in your hand, make others follow you. Don't allow your weakness for getting things in the wrong perspective dominate you. You could get something organised that would grow too big for you. Start in a small way. Feel your powers accumulating within you. Then aim for higher things.

CHIEF CAPABILITIES

An ability to mimic. To appreciate a situation almost immediately. To sympathise with others and to feel with—and for—them. While you may not exactly have a good head for figures, your organising abilities could be put to good use. Provided you left the real headaches for others to sort out.

PET PHOBIA

"Hematophobia"—fear of blushing. You don't blush very often—but you *have* been caught out from time to time. As a social figure, popular, magnetic, you let yourself down by blushing. But your true fear lies in fear that you *will*. Tell yourself you will *not* blush. This simple rule works wonders.

BEST COURSE OF ACTION IN LIFE

Go straight for all you want. But consider others on the way. Tell yourself there is little you cannot achieve in life if you go all out for it. By controlling your habit of making things seem bigger than they are, and by putting a stop to the rise and fall in your career to date, you will stand a fine chance of getting what you want from life.

POSSIBLE PEAK AGE OF POWER

Middle thirties. If you are over thirty—aim for forty-five or thereabouts. Certainly by the age of sixty-five to seventy you should have realised most of your ambitions, but you have every hope of being considerably active to the end of your life! Virility and the desire for progress pin-point the Capricornian—all along the line.

Your PSYCHO-TYPE is magnetic, impulsive, go-ahead, ambitious, generous. Head-in-the-air from time to time. Trustworthy and loyal. Sure of social success in the long run.

11th House

11th Sign of the Zodiac

AQUARIUS

January 21—February 19

SATURN
Ruling Planet

WEAK CHARACTER POINTS

An over-anxious personality. This gets on other people's nerves. You fear fire, water, having accidents, going to hospital. Given the chance, you would suffer from lots of imagined ills of mind and body. Not because you wanted to so much as because you fear the worst—and would like to experience these 'conditions' to prove to yourself they are not so bad as you imagine them to be. You seek to 'inoculate' yourself against the unknown.

STRONG CHARACTER POINTS

You may unconsciously possess healing powers. This is the best way *to* have them because you do not seek to commercialise them. Therefore you could do a great deal of good. A soothing manner, powers of persuasion, gentle hands —could help others who might look to you for assistance.

Considerable powers of discrimination help you to make the right sort of friends, to make correct decisions at the right times. As far as circumstances are concerned, you are adaptable and fall in well with other people's ideas. Your intuition sometimes reaches great heights, so much so that your friends and relatives are sometimes quite mystified. Perhaps you are a little over-sensitive, get easily hurt, turn other people's remarks inwards until they seem to be directed to you alone. A slight persecution-complex, bred in you from the start, makes life an uphill job at times. Try being a bit more hard-boiled. It will pay off. Those around you are far softer and more generous hearted than you would like to think. You are kind to children, old people and animals. Sometimes you are willing to sacrifice your own happiness for the sake of others. This is not always a wise policy. Others are apt to think you are soft. Try being a little more hard hearted as well as hard boiled. You have an in-born sense of the fitness of things. You can be depended upon to be cool and calm in a crisis and to be able to put others at their ease.

DOMINANT AMBITIONS

Always to do good to others. To see the other person's point of view. But this makes you all too pliable in the hands of schemers. You do not possess any particular material ambition. You could be a drifter if it were not for the inborn urge to be of help. This is a saving grace in an otherwise rather effortless life. You feel there is something at the end of a long road to which you cannot quite reach out. This may be a source of concern from time to time. Take others into your confidence a bit more. They might easily be able to show you the way.

CHIEF CAPABILITIES

Your ability to adjust to circumstances. Modest, you could command attention in a group, organise people and take on certain important responsibilities. Not necessarily concerned with cash, however, as you are not quite as business-like as you would like to be. You may be methodical, but caution makes you too slow.

PET PHOBIA

"Algophobia"—fear of pain. This arises from extreme sensitivity. Half the time your fear lies in the fact that you are able to 'feel' for others. You transfer *their* feelings, fantasies and fears to yourself until you get quite obsessed by them. Cease thinking inwardly and you should, by and by, get rid of this very common phobia.

BEST COURSE OF ACTION IN LIFE

Think before you look, speak or act. Remember a little thought is always vitally necessary before you give way to impulse. Try being 'top dog' for a change, once in a while. You will gain a great deal of respect that is owing to you. Experiment a little with your dormant healing powers. Provided you do not try to make too much of them and certainly do not turn them into cash profit—you should surprise yourself—and your friends and the family.

POSSIBLE PEAK AGE OF POWER

Assuming you are twenty or thereabout, you should have about five years to go before things really get going. If you are thirty or over, it is about time you were in the swim and really getting somewhere. If that is not the case, and you *are* in your thirties, start thinking really hard. Time is on the wing—and you have a great deal to do in life, many things to accomplish.

Your PSYCHO-TYPE is retiring, up to a point. 'On the job' if a good enough spur is egging you on. You are fair and square and would do no one any serious wrong. You may be a bit head-in-the-air but are able to come down to earth when necessary.

12th House

12th Sign of the Zodiac

PISCES

JUPITER
Ruling Planet

February 20—March 20

WEAK CHARACTER POINTS

You lack knowledge of human nature. This makes you victim to the wiles of others who seek to make you a scapegoat. You are liable to misplace confidence, getting yourself into hot water on more than one occasion. An unstinting desire to give all you have is losing you a lot of respect from others. Be careful it does not cause you to lose respect for yourself also. Get to know a few more sophisticated people who will help lift you out of a rather simple way of life you pursue at the moment. You are a good sort but have a certain weakness of character that will keep you in the background if you are not very careful.

STRONG CHARACTER POINTS

A few more years may well reveal a strong artistic strain in you. But don't force the issue. It will reveal itself to you in a surprising manner. This artistic streak makes you a strong minded person. You see beauty in almost everything. This makes you tolerant and sympathetic, and extremely sensitive. A sense of responsibility will make you a good parent, will help you through many a difficult time in your work-life. Good at figures, people can look to you to strike a good bargain, to look after their affairs if you should be asked to. Children can depend on you for a great deal of true, genuine affection. A certain vision helps you to see ahead more quickly than can the average person. This quality may tend to embarrass at times, for people are not always able to keep up with you. In fact, many disbelieve things you tell them, dismissing them as impossible. But you are proved right in almost every case. There have been times when your rather uncanny money-sense has tended to make you a little bit tight-fisted—especially with those you most love. You have a generous nature and must not let the lure of cash get the upper hand. You are more interested in saving than in spending, but this could get to the point where you might well begin to be a bit miserly. So don't be afraid to go to town a little from time to time.

DOMINANT AMBITIONS

A lurking desire to be top-dog in almost everything you do. This will not always prove to be popular with others, however. You could try to divert your ambitions into other, less egotistical directions. That artistic flair is always tempting you to creative endeavours. That is the main 'itch' you have in life. Could it be in the field of literature—or painting, or are you likely to become a musician? Once again, this is in the stars—for the future to unfold. Enough to know that you have a deep desire to leave your mark on the world in spite of the rather mundane existence you lead at the moment and the simple sort of people you cultivate as friends.

CHIEF CAPABILITIES

A head for figures. Certain intuition. You are a visionary. There is a conflict between the material things in life and the more idealistic aspects. You have a capacity for being practical but find this rather onerous from time to time. Fantasy amuses and attracts you far more than fact. But life sometimes demands facts and will not tolerate idealism and an airy philosophy. Come down to earth—there is so much in you waiting to come out.

PET PHOBIA

"Hamartophobia"—fear of failure. This is because you do not know for sure in which direction to go and you fear that your final choice may be the wrong one. So you persist in being afraid you will be a failure. This is what prevents you deciding between the artistic, idealistic life and the more practical side.

BEST COURSE OF ACTION IN LIFE

Be more decisive. After all, what does it matter what past influences have done to you? Maybe there were parents, teachers or friends who tried to hold you back, tried to convince you it was safer to play life 'straight'—not to be too venturesome. Feet firmly on the ground probably meant you were to go through life being content with the simple things. That is why your associates are not, at present, out of the top intellectual drawer. Dismiss the past. This is *now*. Follow your creative bent. Be practical in all you do. Invest a little cash in your future.

POSSIBLE PEAK AGE OF POWER

Some artists, writers, composers and individualists have not reached *their* success peak until well after middle age. This may well be the case with *you*. The gathering clouds of achievement are slow moving. But you must keep up with them all the time. Probably the late 'fifties will see you really come into your own. By that time you will have assumed a great deal of responsibility. This you will find to be the 'thrust' for which you have been looking—the final inspiration calculated to make you realise your fondest dreams.

Your PSYCHO-TYPE is indecisive, procrastinating, hesitant. Some might analyse this as an inferiority complex. This is not true. Caution is not necessarily confusion. You are the type who bewilders others and frightens them off. That is why the more simple folk gather round you. They are not forced to think hard when with you. Your rock-bottom type is, however, the individualist.

1st House

1st Sign of the Zodiac

ARIES

MARS
Ruling Planet

March 21—April 20

WEAK CHARACTER POINTS

A quick temper does not make you too popular, though people may not make this apparent to your face. You fly off the handle at the slightest excuse and do not give others a chance to explain themselves first. You condition yourself to negative situations and circumstances. Many times, you create them when they otherwise would not exist at all. You also have a capricious nature where affairs of the heart are concerned. This does not help you to be able to plumb the depths of human emotions as much as you would like to. People fight shy of getting too fond of you. They know they will be in great danger of being hurt. This desire to flirt with other people's feeling could lead you into trouble one day. So watch it.

STRONG CHARACTER POINTS

Executive ability should take you a long way where career is concerned. A great spirit of determination may lose you a few friends, but a driving force will spur you on, despite this. Those with whom you deal will be struck by your great earnestness. This is the quality that will mostly endear them to you. Socially, you are able to switch on a genial nature. This may be rather artificial, but only very discerning people will see through you. Provided you do not play fast and loose with them they will rally round and, generally, do your bidding. You have the gift of delegating work to others. You prefer glossing over detail and leaving the intricate matters to underlings. It is conceivable you will make one or two young people prôtégés of yours and they may benefit much from your teaching. While generally smart in your appearance you tend to neglect it from time to time. As a potential executive—(if you are not one already) you need to watch your personal appearance very closely. You have a particularly strong will. Some might consider you pig-headed. This is because you do not temper reason and logic with impulse and hot-headedness.

DOMINANT AMBITIONS

To have a lot of people working for you. This, you are likely to get—to a certain extent. You also wish to be the masterful member of any union you make or may have made. There is a side of your nature that seeks deep affection. You will search a great deal until you find this. You aspire to be much loved, but are you ready to give equal love in return?

This is debatable in the light of your determination to get to the top—and to stay there.

CHIEF CAPABILITIES

Quick-on-the-uptake. An ability to dramatise conditions, circumstances and situations. This gives a rosy hue, in some cases, to otherwise morbid situations, but gives you a rather wry sense of humour that others are quick to appreciate. Broaden your outlook and your sense of fun will bring more friends to your house.

PET PHOBIA

"Monophobia"—fear of being alone. Because you yearn so much for power and the means by which you can satisfactorily express yourself, you seek to be surrounded, as much as possible—by people. Not necessarily by those of your own level, but, for the sake of companionship, you will accept almost anyone who will help inflate your ego. Fight this. Solitude does one good for a while—from time to time. You are the sort who needs to think, at regular intervals. You tend to cramp your style by running away from yourself and your own company so much.

BEST COURSE OF ACTION IN LIFE

Count ten more times than you do now. This way you will make more friends and keep them much longer. Try to be a little more sincere. Being shallow won't get you as far as you want to go. While pursuing your ambitions as well as possible, making as much possible progress you aim to make— keep an eye on those in your immediate circle. Watch carefully how mounting achievement on your part affects them. You have many staunch hangers-on—they would like to share in your happiness. See you take them into consideration.

POSSIBLE PEAK AGE OF POWER

You make hard work of most things, so it may take several years before the sweet smell of success reaches your nostrils. Thirty should see you on your way. If you are thirty already, and there do not seem to be many signs of immediate success —analyse your life up to date in the light of what you have done so far, and find out what has gone wrong. You are all set for success eventually—but certainly, thirty years of age will be enough to have made an auspicious start. Suppose you are well over thirty—in your forties or fifties? There is still time, though it would seem in those circumstances, you have been letting things slip through your fingers a bit too much. Overhaul yourself, and pay stricter attention to essentials.

Your PSYCHO-TYPE is rather bombastic, egotistical, self-centred. Some people interpret this as a go-ahead nature—but you should know better. It means you are putting others before yourself. Try not to be so over-bearing. You are essentially a success-figure provided you retain your sense of proportion.

2nd House

2nd Sign of the Zodiac

TAURUS

VENUS
Ruling Planet

April 21—May 21

WEAK CHARACTER POINTS

Mainly, you find it difficult to save money. Spending it for effect is another weakness. You think you can easily buy favours. If you *do,* they are not genuine. They are as shallow as are your intentions. You have luxurious tastes. You do your best to indulge them—sometimes to your dismay, for rarely do they turn out as good as you first thought they would. You go a great deal by surface appearances. You are not willing to go deep down and find real truths beneath the surface. This way, you don't exactly get the very best life has to offer. Because you form strong likes and dislikes, others are apt to find you a little disconcerting. It would be wise for you to try not to be quite so self-opinionated. Make allowances for others. They like to form judgements, too.

They do not want to always take *your* word. Again, you have an overwhelming desire to dominate, especially members of your opposite sex. This won't do at all, either in married life or in the single state.

STRONG CHARACTER POINTS

Fearlessness is your middle name. This may get you into trouble some day if not properly controlled. This is not exactly courage. It is more a type of bravado. For instance, you would not hesitate to scale a pretty formidable-looking cliff—provided you had an audience to watch your feat of daring. On the other hand, you would not hesitate to go to the rescue of a child, an animal or an adult were you to see them in great danger. So there is good and bad in this quality of yours. Train it along the right lines, however. On more than one occasion you have suspected you possess clairvoyant powers. This may well be true. If it is, use them in the right directions. It is all too easy to do bad things with such a gift. Try to divert this sense of 'seeing' into useful channels. There are many ways of helping others out of their difficulties. You are probably especially sensitive to dangerous vibrations. Your fearlessness arises from this. In everything you do you display great enthusiasm. This, you are easily able to convey to others. In a way, this does a great deal of good. Courage and conviction are contagious. Beware, however, of letting others sap your mental and physical vitality. You are apt to 'give out' a lot. People can 'feed' on your visionary prowess.

DOMINANT AMBITIONS

About these you are rather vague. You really need someone in your life to show you where you are going. There is a great deal you would like to cram into your life—but you feel you have not enough time in which to do everything. That of course, is incorrect. Life lasts a long time on average. Try getting yourself sorted out. Members of the family will not be much help to you. You need to find a true, sincere friend of the opposite sex. If you are married, this might present some problems. But since there will be no emotional content in such a relationship—no complications should arise. Of one thing however, you are perfectly sure, and that is that you want to amount to something. You do not want to leave this life without having made something of a definite impact. What exactly that *is* only time will reveal.

CHIEF CAPABILITIES

Your sense of 'seeing'. Coupled with sensitivity and a great love for humanity in general. You do not get this over to all people, however. You should try approaching your friends on their levels. They have not all got your intellectual approach to life. Certainly, you are apt to choose material folk as your main companions. Because of that—you sometimes suffer from a great sense of loneliness.

PET PHOBIA

"Pathophobia"—fear of suffering. Not so much your own personal mental or physical suffering as that of others. Your fearlessness is translated into terms of hating all pain, all mental anguish on the part of others.

BEST COURSE OF ACTION IN LIFE

To form an intellectual group outside of working hours in which you can find full and free expression. As far as your job in life is concerned, it is doubtful if this will ever be a source of inspiration to you. So just accept it as a means to an end, a way of living, to do good to others when occasion permits. The big things in life you hope to do will stem only from your spare-time activities.

POSSIBLE PEAK AGE OF POWER

Probably this will never be reached, for your way through life will be fraught with doubts—mainly about yourself. It will be your closest, most sincere friends who will be the best judges of your accomplishments. Probably, in very old age, you will be able to look back, and pin-point many successes here and there that will stand out as peak-ages in your life. There will be no grand climax—no leading-up point. Your name is more likely to mean something when it is just a memory.

Your PSYCHO-TYPE is ethereal, delicate in the intellectual sense. Idealism occupies a deal of your time. So you are given to day dreams. You are the organising type, provided you meet the right, sympathetic people. A certain amount of egotism tends to make you overbearing. Your inability to save money makes you something of an eccentric, but not one to be laughed at. You are rather a special sort of person, and only appreciated completely by those who are your kindred spirits.

3rd House

3rd Sign of the Zodiac

GEMINI

MERCURY
Ruling Planet

May 22—June 21

WEAK CHARACTER POINTS

A moody person, you are up one minute and down the next. Is this good? A bit perplexing to those around you. They find it difficult to keep up with you. You are a little too proud. Not vain, but proud in a haughty way. This is due to a certain amount of inner inferiority—a sense of inadequacy. Unfounded, in fact, for you are really quite a clever person all round. You have a nervy disposition in that you 'scatter' your nervous energy in all directions instead of concentrating it all on one focal point and making a one hundred per-cent good job of any jobs in hand. You are also somewhat of an extremist. You magnify most things and make them far harder work than they need be. Where the opinions of others are concerned, you have a tendency to read false meanings into them. You willingly and deliberately distort criticism, and many times turn praise inward so that you can put a malignant meaning into it. This is to hurt yourself—for often you enjoy wallowing in self-pity. A great mistake, because, were you to come out of this silly shell, you could do a great lot of good in the world and might well amount to something quite significant.

STRONG CHARACTER POINTS

An affectionate nature draws others to you—but as you have just read, you drive them away again in many cases. Try to develop this affectionate nature more, and get more fun out of it. You are in a position to attract the right sort of folk to you. Why not make the most of this quality? Coupled with this, you are sympathetic—yet another quality others admire in you. You have deep religious convictions but are unable to follow an accepted line of thought in this direction. This does not matter so very much, as your true faith in Providence covers a multitude of doubts. You have an unselfish nature until such times as you start turning your thoughts inwards. You could mean a lot of things to a lot of people if only you would let yourself go a bit more. As far as beauty is concerned, you have considerable powers of discernment in regard to the arts. Pictures, music, sculpture, beautiful scenery, design and display all come under your notice. You are able cleverly to analyse and construct. If you have not any particular aptitude to create anything of your own— your critical faculties are of help to others who seek your advice. It might not be a bad idea to try to find out if you have, in fact, some unsuspected creative outlet. A restless nature is not to be condemned. This gives you a spirit of adventure.

DOMINANT AMBITIONS

To be jack of many trades, and master of most of them at the same time. A rather impossible and idle ambition. This is due mainly to the fact that you scatter your abilities and fail to concentrate on any one in particular. The key to success as far as you are concerned is to *specialise*. There is one thing you should be able to do really well. Go out of your way to find this. If you can stop being quite so temperamental you will soon settle down and be on the way to being somebody.

CHIEF CAPABILITIES

A highly colourful imagination and artistic appreciation. An interest in many subjects. A drive deep down inside that will not, in the long run, be denied. This is quite a marvellous gift. Not many possess it. But there is the negative quality of temperament holding you back. Overcome this. Socially, you have it in you to be brilliant. At work, you could well become a leader. In the home, you could be the source of great happiness and harmony.

PET PHOBIA

"Nyctophobia"—fear of darkness. This is not only a physical fear. You fear darkness of mind. You are afraid the day may come when you can no longer appreciate the brilliance of beauty, the light of artistic comprehension. In a dark room, this fear grows in proportion to the physical awareness of material dark. Always live and sleep where there is some little light at least. This will help your mental attitude.

BEST COURSE OF ACTION IN LIFE

To try to discover your dominant personality and then to go all out to develop it on the right lines. To find your real forté and stick to it. Try to get rid of foolish feelings of imagined persecution. You only tend to bring the thing into being. When religious convictions conflict—be thankful you have the gift of faith. So many have not. Pursue a more steady course in life and don't use up so much nervous energy in useless directions.

POSSIBLE PEAK AGE OF POWER

If you are young—you may suddenly make a great impact on your contemporaries and confound those who tend to look on you rather as an oddity. On the other hand, if you are well on the way to your thirties or forties, experience will mellow you and a certain degree of sophistication will stand you in good stead and steer you to success in your middle fifties. Many personalities such as you have broken the ice at quite an advanced age. That is quite likely where you are concerned. Small triumphs all along the line will encourage you to greater, more powerful things later.

Your PSYCHO-TYPE is mildly Schizophrenic (don't be frightened). This only means, in your case—changeable. You are indeterminate, varied in outlook, possessor of many capabilities. Emotional, and likely to carry others along with you on a tide of unrestricted emotionalism from time to time. You are likeable, more or less, because some people welcome the individualist. But, to some others, you appear as a bundle of nerves and are not very good for them. You upset their serenity of mind and spoil their conservative outlook.

4th House

4th Sign of the Zodiac

CANCER

June 22—July 23

MOON
Ruling Planet

WEAK CHARACTER POINTS

You are rather a solitary sort of person. You could well be described as anti-social. Not from necessity by any means. You could have plenty of popularity, but you have a strong tendency to turn inwards. Introspection is your weakest point. Tomorrow means more to you than today, and you do not concern yourself enough *with* tomorrow. You have a fondness for money and, having got a little together, prefer to look at it rather than spend it. This does not amount to wise thrift. Rather is it a tendency to be miserly and ungenerous. You possess a mechanical mind. If you do not pursue a career that calls for the use of your hands and the possession of an enquiring mind, you could well use such capabilities to some advantage were you to wish for a change of occupation. You wake each morning on top of the world, but by evening you are down in the dumps. This is your average daily way of behaviour. The line of least resistance attracts you more than immediate, positive action. This is a great weakness you acknowledge but to which you give way a great deal too much.

STRONG CHARACTER POINTS

You have strong will power. This comes from keeping to yourself so much and having to fend for yourself. It does not, however, win you many admirers. You have powers of intuition. Use them more to your advantage. You could be of considerable use to others in advising them. You also have the makings of a good speaker.

DOMINANT AMBITIONS

You must confess, truthfully, you do not know quite *where* you are going. Indecision prevents your making up your mind. Your love of being alone prevents full expansion of your personality. It might be true to say that you want to be a lone figure in some highly specialised field in which you are an authority. But you want no interference from others. You also want to make a lot of money to bank against insecurity. This sense of impending insecurity arises from an inner insecurity of *mind*. That, in turn, comes from your inability to get outside of yourself and to share your life with others. What can you do? Thwarted ambition is an awkward thing with which to live. Examine well your mechanical turn of mind. Look at your hands and ask yourself what best you can do with them. The worker with hands is usually a sort of solitary type—for there is much time for thought when the hands are moving automatically in the creation of something mechanical.

CHIEF CAPABILITIES

Money-making sense provided you do not waste the end product. Strength of mind which, if put in the right direction, could do you a great deal of good.

PET PHOBIA

"Ochlophobia"—fear of crowds. This results from your liking for solitude. It is a self-induced state of mind and should be conquered. Mix more. Force yourself to enter a social circle. Dramatics, rambles, organised games would do you a great deal of good. You also suffer from another 'phobia'—"Xenophobia"—fear of strangers. All part and parcel of your absurd love of being alone. This also ties up with your desire to make money and to keep it to yourself. Try spending some of it on others. People rarely remain strangers for long once they have had some money spent on them. Money opens the door to many places. Make a very special note of these two anti-social 'phobias' from which you suffer. They are holding you back seriously.

BEST COURSE OF ACTION IN LIFE

Perhaps the most important quality you should cultivate is that of tolerance. Lack of tolerance may well be the reason why you like to keep yourself to yourself so much. You are too lazy to consider others. You have no time to spare for what other people feel and think. You do not wish to enter into their lives, and certainly you have no patience, sympathy or tolerance with them. So try to *be* more tolerant with those in your immediate circle, however restricted this may be because of your own attitude to life. Life is meant to be shared with other people. One only half lives if one does *not* live with—and for—others, as well.

POSSIBLE PEAK AGE OF POWER

Because of your rather immature outlook and undeveloped social sense, it is not possible to suggest any particular time of life in which you will be able to reach a pitch of achievement that could be called in any way—successful. Everything depends on how soon you are able to grow up mentally and assume the adult responsibilities of caring for and living for others as well as for yourself.

Your PSYCHO-TYPE is emotionally undeveloped. You are not, in the strictest sense—mature or adult, whatever age you happen to be. However, all these things are under the control of ourselves, in spite of the fact we are blessed—or cursed—with tendencies that are, in some cases, unfortunate. You can snap out of the type of person you are, and, though you will, of course, retain the dominant characteristics with which you have been born, there is every hope you can make a success of yourself in the long run and change your outlook for the better. An emotionally undeveloped type such as yourself often has many compensating qualities which are not always too hard to find.

5th House

5th Sign of the Zodiac

LEO

July 24—August 23

SUN
Ruling Planet

WEAK CHARACTER POINTS

Lazy, indolent, tomorrow will do. Easily influenced by others. Your money-sense is not well developed. You would sooner borrow from others than make your own cash. Indecisive attitudes to life make it hard for you to be a positive force in matters that mean quick thinking and immediate action.

STRONG CHARACTER POINTS

Generous to the extreme where it comes to sharing personal possessions, not cash. But you will share money at times, after you have got it from some source or other that has not meant hard work. Mainly you will be willing *to* share it to help you overcome a sense of guilt over the way in which you have acquired it. You are a gullible person, with a quick tongue and will know the right thing to say to suit your own ends. People describe you as 'plausible'. But you are extremely loyal, and, in your devil-may-care way, rarely let your friends down. With a little development and a little good advice from others, you could be quite a social asset provided it was never left to you to make final decisions. Specially in the catering line, either socially or from a career point of view, you could be quite successful. You have a pleasant knack of knowing what foods go with what—and could lay a good table. This amounts to a domestic sense as well as, from that point of view, you could please many people. You also have the ability to inspire others. Possibly, because you are so care-free, they feel they also can be happy in life by adopting a similar attitude. It does not always work out so well for them—however. You are a soothing influence on your friends also, and they will seek you out in times of trouble. You are likeable, lovable to many.

DOMINANT AMBITIONS

You have few. Just to be content, happy as the day is long. Perhaps there is a lurking desire to be the centre of attraction or to be someone upon whom others have to depend a great deal. This comes from your strong domestic instincts. You are not exactly cut out as a career-figure but, without doubt you know you are meant to mean *something* to someone. Your desires in life are vague. You have a happy disposition. Possibly you are happiest when you are making those around you happy too.

CHIEF CAPABILITIES

An inborn sense of fun and the ability to make light of most troubles. A good philosophy of life could make existence pretty happy for you.

PET PHOBIA

Because you have a lot of time on your hands in which to think, you are apt to be rather a hypochondriac—(one who imagines he has a lot of diseases or conditions of ill-health). You therefore acknowledge a fear of quite a few things. At rock bottom, however, you are rather too open-minded to let these 'fears' get the better of you. You are inclined to admit to them only when you are feeling intellectually starved, and are finding yourself—instead of others—the more interesting study of the moment. In such times, you would readily admit to "Peccatophobia"—fear of sinning. A prevalent feeling of guilt that you are taking advantage of life prompts you to feel you commit sins of omission (things you fail to do). At other times—you suffer from "Acrophobia"—fear of high places. This last is very deeply psychological. You fear being placed on a pedestal by your friends—and being able to live up to their high opinions of you. You feel you would be inadequate and would disappoint them. You will also confess, from time to time, to a fear of death—"Thanatophobia" —a quite unnatural and unnecessary dislike of funerals, operations, suffering and all forms of unhappiness. This can be analysed as a fear of the cessation of your peculiar and particular way of life, pursued, as it is, on easy-come-easy-go lines. You are jealous of your outlook on life and are afraid it may, one day, be taken away from you.

BEST COURSE OF ACTION IN LIFE

To turn your good qualities to good account. To make the most of your devil-may-care attitude so that it does good to others. A vocation in life where you minister to the sick and the needy would be ideal. Provided you did not have any administerial duties whatsoever as you would make a hopeless hash of them.

POSSIBLE PEAK AGE OF POWER

Power is not exactly what you are after. Peace of mind is more your pigeon. This—you have had from an early age—

and will continue to have. You may easily exert great influence over people many years your junior when you reach middle-age. If you never amount to anything particularly spectacular, you will go down as having been a jolly good sort. You will bring a lot of joy into people's lives.

Your PSYCHO-TYPE is difficult to define. Only your closest friends could adequately sum you up. Enough to say you are quite rare as a personality, easy to live with but quite exasperating from time to time.

6th House

6th Sign of the Zodiac

VIRGO

MERCURY
Ruling Planet

August 24—September 23

WEAK CHARACTER POINTS

Watch a desire to dominate and get the last word in—even if it isn't the best word. You lose friends because you are too keen to criticise—too often. You like the best things in life but perhaps are not too prepared to work too hard to get them. A fastidious nature is apt to get on other people's nerves.

STRONG CHARACTER POINTS

Methodical. You finish a job once you start it. But beware of this becoming a compulsion. You have the makings of a perfectionist. This trait can sometimes get out of proportion and end in making the most trivial of tasks a great, looming responsibility. You have a scholarly turn of mind. Knowledge is your business—at least—in spare time. But you should apply this useful tendency also to your job in life. People are well able to depend on you though you force your will once you have been given a job of work to do. You have a marked appreciation for good music. An eye for colour and design.

Intellectual companions find you most refreshing. Revolutionary ideas you bring to bear on present-day problems might be met by opposition—but they prove good food for thought for your immediate circle. In career—you are go-ahead. Most likely to succeed because of a great sense of responsibility and an ability to be authoritative in the right direction. Some of your closest friends have detected certain psychic powers you do not perhaps as yet know you possess. You also have an aptitude for calming those in trouble, for soothing the troubled breast.

DOMINANT AMBITIONS

To attain an executive position in your chosen career. To be well respected, looked-up to. Considered an authority in that in which you particularly specialise. A position of some merit in your social sphere is also not beyond your hopes and expectations. Or ability to attain.

CHIEF CAPABILITIES

Your ability to carry through a job from its beginning to its logical end. Continuity of thought is one of your greatest assets. And you are not easily swayed by the opinions of others. In a way—this can be a fault—for the self-opinionated person is rarely popular. However, provided you allow for the opinion of others when it happens to be the right one—you will not go far wrong. Your individuality of thought is also useful to you. In a sometimes conservative world—a little bit of originality goes places. You are also able to command. You have a sense of authority that brings respect. Your psychic powers will best keep for social contacts. Healing has never been lucrative—though a most blessed vocation.

PET PHOBIA

You are lucky enough to possess no particular phobia. You rather tend to suffer from mild compulsions to be always up and doing—all of the time. This could, at a stretch, be analysed as "Harmartophobia"—fear of failure. But that would not be consistent with your go-aheadness. People who fear personal failure rarely make day-to-day efforts to succeed and to lead.

BEST COURSE OF ACTION IN LIFE

Try to control your impetuous nature. More friends will be made—and kept—by checking your enormous reserves of driving force. Learn as much as you can absorb, but do your best to concentrate on a specific course of action. Too much learning might eventually confuse you and you would end by getting nowhere at all—after all.

POSSIBLE PEAK AGE OF POWER

You have matured at an early age. Progress will not seem so swift since you are, at the moment, forging ahead, perhaps unknown to yourself. If a point is to be reached when the *ultimate* will have been reached—it should occur about the middle forties. Socially you can expect to be something of a figure before the thirties—or just after. Not, however, by virtue of your psychic powers. These will be conserved for very special uses—among your intimates—and those who turn to you for help.

Your PSYCHO-TYPE is intellectual. You talk great good sense, but a lot of it is above the heads of the man-in-the-street. But you force your ideas quite violently upon others. You are also a marked artistic type, but flounder in a complex circle of indecision as to medium of expression. Generally, you are a colourful person to know, disconcerting to many, but definitely interesting. A type to be sought out. You stand out in a crowd.

7th House

7th Sign of the Zodiac

LIBRA

VENUS
Ruling Planet

September 24—October 23

WEAK CHARACTER POINTS

A speculative nature makes you rather a bad bet as far as cash is concerned. You enjoy a risk here and there—which

is not always successful. Apart from that—you sometimes like
to gamble with human emotions. This puts others in a spot
for they are not always able to adjust themselves to your
changes of mood or to accept your fickle behaviour. You also
have a reckless nature. Speed, excitement, adventure all add
up to living it up for you. Others who are not able to keep
the pace retire, baffled. This does not make for happy social
or work-time associations. The family, also, are prone to
suffer from anxiety as to your next moves. On the other
hand, you have moments of being very sensitive, easily hurt.
You are likely to twist statements and criticisms until they
are turned in against you. Normally, this is untrue and you
bring more hurt to yourself than has been intended. You
have a rather calculating nature which your friends take to
show lack of feeling. The mathematics of a thing interest
you more, at times, than considerations for the human
element.

STRONG CHARACTER POINTS

Vastly ambitious, you could drive yourself hard. Very
perceptive and little escapes you. This gift should be turned
to your career and not used as a weapon against your friends.
You have an orderly mind with a strong streak of domesticity. Extreme optimism carries you through life on the
crest of a wave—but beware of being too confident. Temper
your moves with the utmost discretion. Let your powers of
perception lead you. While, from time to time, you display
an innate sense of justice in dealing with your fellow-men, you
do, at times, go off the rails and seriously *misjudge*. This
helps make enemies. Apt to be an extremist. This is good
to a point for it helps you to see beyond the horizon to possible pitfalls that may lie ahead. Be careful, however, not to
mix fantasy with fact and to let the extreme view triumph
over the rational.

DOMINANT AMBITIONS

To make life as exciting as possible. To have varied,
exciting adventures. To be all-powerful in the social and
industrial scene. You have a strong creative urge but, lacking
the right mode of expression—you dabble in many things.
You have a great desire to be an individualist. A lot of money
is not exactly your main aim. Notoriety would be nearer the

mark. In the best possible way, of course. You might easily find a sense of inferiority behind this great urge to stand out in a crowd.

CHIEF CAPABILITIES

A glib tongue that should be well-guarded on occasion. Insight, that could be turned to very good use. A cool, calculating attitude that should be developed along business lines.

PET PHOBIA

"Insectophobia"—fear of insects. This is not very highly developed. Its origin is traceable to a horror of meanness and petty-mindedness. Your 'insects' are small-minded people, insignificant affairs that cause worry and unnecessary anxiety. You abhor anything that is creepy, crawling, slow moving. This is the direct opposite to the speed with which you wish to order your life. Insects represent repression and inhibition to you. You stamp on them or swat them, and, in so doing, hit out at your imagined or real, imperfections, This fear of your inner self translates itself in terms of abhorrence of insects, with which may also be included rats and mice. As with many, you fear the unknown more than the creatures themselves. Face up to yourself more, and this un-reasoning phobia may well disappear.

BEST COURSE OF ACTION IN LIFE

Come down to earth more. Allow your dealings with others to have more of the human element. Less risky speculations and more concrete, well-thought out moves on your part will bring more success your way in the long run. Be less of a victim to self pity and stop twisting what people have to say to you if it does not happen to be all praise—all of the time. Live at a slower pace generally. Exchange your love of speed in thought and action for the slower, more calculated, more reasonable way of life. That way—people will be able to catch up with you and stay the pace. It follows that you will then get far more out of them to your lasting benefit.

PEAK AGE OF POWER

Is there one for you? Living at your present pace—you are liable to burn yourself up. Peak power may never be reached mentally, though, of course, you will go on living on dreams. Dreams, however, will not be enough for you. Possibly, with care over your attitude to life, you could amount to quite a lot in your middle years, when maturity has caught up with you and sobered you down a little. Although your life expectations are good—beware of using up so much mental energy that later could and should be put to good account when triumphs in your life *really* matter.

Your PSYCHO-TYPE is complex. Emotionally highly strung, quick tempered. Imaginative, quite an actor or actress, you look upon the world as your stage. A false sense of values many times lets you down. You are, generally, an enigma to most of your friends. Erratic, sensitive, your feelings are easily swayed one moment, firmly fixed the next.

8th House

8th Sign of the Zodiac

SCORPIO

MARS
Ruling Planet

October 24—November 22

WEAK CHARACTER POINTS

Very prone to be highly influenced by flattery. An exhibitionist, in the nicest possible sense. Always 'on stage'. Always ready to play to the gallery. You also procrastinate to the point of exasperation. This is due to an over-developed sense of your own importance and significance.

STRONG CHARACTER POINTS

You possess great mental and physical vitality. You have an aptitude to deny illness and mental stress and strain. Because of this—it hardly exists in your life at all. You have a strong will power, and you exert this on others as much as you can. You also use it on yourself to great advantage. Powers of observation are very highly developed. This finds adequate outlet in modes of self-expression such as writing, painting, composing, dancing. You are also a good speaker. In conversation—eloquent and rarely at a loss for words. You are also a good listener, sometimes from boredom (especially if you are having to take a back seat for a while). But usually you are able to convince that you really *are* interested—and therefore get away with it. You are the essence of tact when called for. But sometimes, the discerning are apt to see through your façade—and to translate your 'tact' in terms of cynicism or sarcasm. You have plenty of confidence in all you undertake in life, socially, business-wise and in your domestic sphere. You possess poise and are a master of pose. People find you affable when you are in a good mood and being pleased. When, however, you are crossed, people have to beware of your biting tongue. You accept challenges with a good will and work until you overcome them. Fond of sport, you win quite a few triumphs.

DOMINANT AMBITIONS

Not to pass through life without making a very definite mark. To enjoy life to the full, to get every full moment of excitement from it. To achieve as much as possible in the shortest space of time. Your extreme vitality and will to win gets you in hot water from time to time with those who cannot keep up with you, or who resent your go-ahead attitude. You are determined to work up to the last moment. Retirement will not be for you—if you can help it.

CHIEF CAPABILITIES

A vivid imagination. A capacity to put yourself in another's place. To appreciate suffering. A great sense of humour. But this sometimes vanishes under the weight of imagined oppression. A forthright manner that calls a spade a spade. An 'enemy-winner' on occasion, but you earn the respect of your associates.

PET PHOBIA

If you have a phobia at all, it is the very opposite to that with which people would credit you. For instance—"Hydrophobia"—fear of water. Or "Hematophobia"—fear of the sight of blood. Not necessarily your own. You may also suffer from "Mysophobia"—fear of dirt and germs. This comes from your desire to be fit and well for as long as possible (in this you greatly succeed). "Toxophobia"—fear of being poisoned, is easily another phobia that might assail you. Due, also, to your almost fanatical desire to be healthy.

BEST COURSE OF ACTION IN LIFE

To go all out for all you aim to get in life. To make good impressions on all with whom you meet up. To be liked on all sides, to be monied, powerful—a name with which to be reckoned.

PEAK AGE OF POWER

Almost any time after your eighteenth birthday. But, more likely than not, you will achieve many 'peaks' and go down from time to time. The 'down' periods will only serve to spur you on to fresh efforts until you reach another phase in life where you are on top.

Your PSYCHO-TYPE is rather confusing to the onlooker who never quite understands what type you *are*. Dominating, moody one moment, up in the air the next, you are the world's problem child. You are the fighter-type, the stuff of which success is made—usually the hard way. People in close touch with you are more or less fascinated by your cheek, appalled, sometimes, by your arrogance, but respect you for your guts when they are not hating them. Your type has always welcomed opposition, upon which it thrives. A deeply religious strain makes you attribute your triumphs and achievements to a Divine Source. This is perhaps all to the good, as it prevents your being completely egotistical. It is also a genuine character-trait, and you get much comfort from it. People who have to live with you are sure of an erratic, exciting time, provided they can stay the pace. Tempestuous, your histrionic ability causes you to live a dramatised life in which most of your associates are supporting players and from whom you are forever taking your cue.

9th House
9th Sign of the Zodiac

SAGITTARIUS

JUPITER
Ruling Planet

November 23—December 22

WEAK CHARACTER POINTS

A secretive nature prevents your making as many friends as you could. You are not always willing to share your trials, troubles and triumphs with others—especially those closest to you. You should realise that there are many around you who would be only too ready and willing to share your ups and downs. An over-cautious nature holds you back. You could go far were you to be a little more adventurous. You find difficulty in dealing with more than one matter at a time.

STRONG CHARACTER POINTS

From time to time you are possessed of quite extraordinary mental and physical energy. Put this to more good use than you do at the moment. You are extremely enterprising, but, due to your tendency of keeping things too much to yourself, you lose many opportunities of breaking fresh ground and really going to town. You are careful with money. Anyone can trust you with their cash, and were you to invest something for someone, your insight into financial matters would turn a little into a lot, a small amount into a good investment. You are not, however, quite so fortunate when it comes to investing money for your own private reasons. People find you strong and courageous. Your strength lies in your seemingly 'strong-man' act, which is in reality, your secretiveness in action. You are, however, strong willed when it comes to the push, and certainly you would be brave in the face of danger. You are also one of those people with powers of intuition, probably this accounts for your good luck with other people's cash. You possess a very strong musical trend. You appreciate almost any type of musical endeavour.

DOMINANT AMBITIONS

To lead a calm, ordered life, without any undue excitements. Domesticity holds a fascination for you—either from the 'handy-man' point of view or from sheer house pride. You want a neat, tidy, ordered household around you as much as you wish for a precise, well-disciplined existence. You wish to be looked up to by your immediate circle, but of course, you rather defeat this by your habit of keeping things too much to yourself. You would like to teach, or to hold some job in which you had students or children under your command. You would rather meet, marry or mix with someone just a little your intellectual inferior. That way—you can do your 'strong-man' act without fear of any very great opposition.

CHIEF CAPABILITIES

A sense of logic. An ability to give strength to others in time of crisis. An appreciation of beauty and the finer things of life. A deep-rooted conviction of righteousness in all you do. You may need to review this from time to time—in case you become too hide-bound by convention and, in an unconservative world—run the risk of being dubbed straight-laced.

PET PHOBIA

"Astraphobia"—fear of thunderstorms. This can be interpreted in other ways. A fear of violence in any shape or form. Of loud noises, explosions, undue brilliance. Consternation. Anything, in fact, that is sudden—for which you are unprepared. Thunderstorms are the symbols of the panic, the disordered circumstance, the mental 'explosion' from which you wish to escape. Yet, with friends in need, you would brave a great deal in any crisis. That is because you are willing to share danger but fear facing up to it on your own.

BEST COURSE OF ACTION IN LIFE

To open out more, mix more, make more friends. To be more of an extrovert and less of an introvert. Take people into your confidence more. Splash out more from time to time. Try to extend your imaginative scope beyond the home.

PEAK AGE OF POWER

May be rather slow going, and you may have a long time to wait. Mainly because of your slow approach to life. A good cash deal you carry out for someone else could be the means of changing your circumstances radically. This could mean a quicker rise to power of some sort or the other. But it depends so very much on yourself, and how soon you can change your attitude and broaden your outlook. The world is full of such as yourself—solid, stolid, reliable—but, a bit of an enigma. The world is a better place for individuals such as yourself, for you help to slow up pace of existence which is always far too fast, anyway. But this does you no immediate good.

Your PSYCHO-TYPE is vague, unless it is said that you are retiring, over-placid, fearful of branching out. A certain amount of inferiority mixed with mistrust of your fellow men makes you a complex type. You do not quite understand yourself.

THE STARS PASS FROM MENTAL TO PHYSICAL

You have now learned your weaknesses, your strong points. Have discovered your dominant ambitions in life. The things at which you are most good. You know what is the phobia of your life—that of which you are most afraid.

The best course of action you can (or should) take in life has been mapped out for you. You can now look forward to the time when you hope to reach your zenith—the time when your mental powers will be at their fullest and best.

You have had your Psycho-Type defined. Don't be put off with the term! It means the psychological type of person you are. The stars have bestowed gifts on you, have given you a few disadvantages. They have made your way of life smooth, or a rough path strewn with many obstacles.

But remember—these are tendencies, pre-dispositions. You *can* make your life run more smoothly if you have a will to. Over all that you do in life, though, will be the ever powerful influences of the Star under which you were born. So, in some cases, in some certain ways of your life, destiny will be in command. But why fear destiny—or try to oppose it?

Many people look back over their life-span and realise how many things *were* planned for them. How they were *made* to make such-and-such a move. How, if they had *not*, life would have been totally different. Probably not so happy. And what of the bad moves, the steps in the wrong direction? Again, destiny must be allowed a say. Out of all bad there comes good.

Study the ZODIACURE next, the health trends shown in your stars. Health is the second most important thing to mental attitude. Learn how to look after yourself after you have read the tendencies and pre-dispositions to good, bad or indifferent health with which you have been blessed with the stars. And, again, take heed of destiny. Do not, if you suffer ill-health, be too discouraged. There is the law of compensation always at work. The sick in body are often brilliant in mind.

Good diets, (especially those based on the natural way of life) are imperative for optimum health. Breathing, relaxing and good exercise are other essentials.

A correct balance of mineral salts is advisable in order

the body's functions may work correctly. All these you will find in the ZODIACURE.

Again, remember, conditions of health and ill-health are tendencies, pre-dispositions. In matters of health, you yourself can do a great deal to overcome minor conditions by living correctly.

The ZODIACURE shows personal health-trends. Tells you what to do to improve your general health. Read your Sun Sign Section in conjunction with your Psycho-Sign, and find a happy medium between your mental and physical existence. Somewhere—between the two points—lies individual success in your personal endeavours throughout life.

After the ZODIACURE comes YOUR STAR AURA. In that section you link your Psycho-Type with your physical type and, from that, get an assessment of your personality-type. You are, in fact, three people. Your Mind-Self, your Body-Self and your Personality-Self. All three types are irrevocably linked. You cannot live to the full without understanding and controlling each individual type.

To this—add luck and good fortune, which you will learn about in the last section—Your Star Sign. Before that, however, you will get to know your Star Make-Up, what you should look like physically. How your emotional life makes out. What your social chances are. How you are likely to progress in your everyday working life.

Now read on. And don't forget to include your friends and family. Only by knowing *their* mental, physical and personality-types can you hope to live with them in harmony, progress with them in business and social life, make allowances for them, understand their little peculiarities. Let them in on *your* star trends too. Then they will begin to understand *you* more!

PART TWO

Your Zodiacure

*Individual Health Guidance from the
Twelve Signs of the Zodiac*

The Sun Signs commence again with December

YOUR ZODIACURE

CAPRICORN
December 23—January 20

CONSTITUTION

A tendency to nervous dyspepsia, stomach troubles. They arise from anxiety, over-doing things at your job, getting overwrought over small things. Bronchial tendencies arise mostly from the same unnecessary expenditure of nervous energy.

DEFICIENCY MINERAL

FERR. PHOS. (Phosphate of Iron). This mineral gives force to the body, strengthens arteries. It also helps bowel-function and has a soothing influence on the digestive tract.

ESSENTIAL VITAMIN-NEEDS

Vitamin B_1 to be found in nuts, fruits, cereals. Aids digestion, gives you a healthy appetite, makes the nerves more steady and helps you to concentrate and memorise.

TRY THIS SPECIAL DIET

No coffee, cocoa or tea for a week. Fresh fruit juices. Plenty of cabbage, spinach, onions. Eggs to give you protein. No soups for a while. Apples, grapes, oranges and pears. Salads of turnip, watercress, celery. Grated carrots, tomatoes. Use olive oil in moderation. Potatoes, for that extra little bit of starch.

YOUR BREATHING EXERCISES

For clarity of thought, your brain must have a constant, and good, supply of oxygenated blood. By breathing well, you guarantee it. Try this . . . Close your mouth. A deep breath should then be taken through the nostrils. Hold for five seconds. Breathe out slowly, through the mouth. This should be done several times a day in front of an open window. If your heartbeats appear to be specially loud and a little fast at the beginning of this exercise—do not be worried. That is the natural outcome of suddenly altering your regular breathing habits. Make a point of carrying out this breathing exercise when you are specially het-up, or when you have a crisis facing you, or when getting ready for a meeting or an appointment that means a great deal to you.

POSSIBLE PEAK AGE OF VIRILITY AND PHYSICAL PERFECTION

Because of your great emotional and nervous output, you will be continually highly-strung. But not to the great detriment of your general health. So fond of living are you that you will decry ill-health. However, reasonable caution must be observed. By the time you are thirty-five or thereabouts, you should be enjoying greatest good health. Your general health picture is that of a highly sensitised organism, supercharged with mental life that draws a great deal upon your physical make-up. You are like a battery that has a constant charge of new current put into it. Be careful, however, that parts do not eventually get too worn away until there is little left to re-charge. If you are past thirty, you should, at the moment, be enjoying physical life to the full. If not, see a doctor to check up.

CAPRICORN—THE GOAT

Healthwise you are stubborn, stoic, strong. But nerve-tautened, straining at the leash, tip-toe at the starting point.

AQUARIUS
January 21—February 19

CONSTITUTION

Vital body heat is sometimes lost through a tendency to periodic despondency. This, in turn, causes poor circulation of the blood stream. The legs, feet and hands are likely to feel the cold. The effect of this on mental effort is, from time to time, to slow up thought and action and to rob you of the power of positive effort.

DEFICIENCY MINERAL

NAT. MUR. (Sodium Chloride). This mineral controls action of the fluids of the body. Poor spirits result from a deficiency of this mineral. That accounts for your periodic bouts of despondency. Your normal physical growth and development is controlled, to a very large degree, by this mineral.

ESSENTIAL VITAMIN-NEEDS

Vitamin B_2 to be found in fish, milk, eggs, cereals, vegetables. This vitamin allays anxiety, contributes towards a calm, reasoned outlook and will help you to follow-through on most problems in life.

TRY THIS SPECIAL DIET

For a week—lemon water, unsweetened. Fresh apples for breakfast. For lunch—pears and oranges. For tea, weak tea and wholemeal bread and butter. Melons, pineapples and peaches will be good as well on this one-week all-fruit diet plus wholemeal-bread-supplement.

YOUR BREATHING EXERCISES

Develop rhythmic control of the abdominal muscles by breathing in through the nose and expanding points above the waist line. This pushes forward the stomach to a small degree and is excellent exercise for the stomach muscles whenever they tend to get flabby and soft. Keep yourself in a good upright standing position as you do this exercise. Breathe in through the nose about a dozen times, slowly and regularly. Make a measured count of one . . . two . . . three as you breathe. This way, you will establish rhythm and your stomach muscles will respond easily and well without undue strain. This exercise will give you inner confidence, will make you more aware of bodily strength, will help you think with more confidence. Breathing correctly is a great controller of scattered, anxious thinking-processes.

POSSIBLE PEAK AGE OF VIRILITY AND PHYSICAL PERFECTION

At a young age, you should be feeling strength of mind and body provided you have developed a positive attitude to life. If you have not, physical perfection may be delayed until middle thirties or even after. You are the sort of person whose physical output is controlled and dominated more by what you think than by what you are. A great deal of delay is caused in your development by poor circulation. This, in turn, comes about by a certain amount of lethargy and apathy on your part. A more vigorous life, more exercise and expenditure of physical energy coupled with more use of a fertile imagination would hasten your Peak Age of Perfection and add considerably to your vitality and vigour.

AQUARIUS—THE WATER CARRIER

Healthwise you are fluid, vibrant, electric, highly sensitised. But emotionally immature at times, thin blooded, weak on the surface.

PISCES
February 20—March 20

CONSTITUTION

Another type to suffer from weak digestive function. Women may have a tendency to uterine difficulties. Actual physical strength, in the strictest sense of the word, is considerable. Powers of endurance are very apparent. The stomach weakness is, in many ways, a compensation, a way out of determined and prolonged physical and mental effort through life. Your body sometimes takes a 'holiday'.

DEFICIENCY MINERAL

FERR. PHOS. (Phosphate of Iron). This mineral

strengthens your blood stream. As you get older, this mineral will be of great benefit. When you find yourself running a temperature for no apparent physical reason, this mineral will help bring it down.

ESSENTIAL VITAMIN-NEEDS

Vitamin D, to be found in fresh milk, eggs, liver oils and cod liver oils. This vitamin aids your personality development and is especially good for tightening up nerves in times of stress and indecision.

TRY THIS SPECIAL DIET

Vegetable broths. Keep away from meat for a week. Make up with potatoes in their jackets, plenty of fresh fruit. Milk or fruit juices to quench the thirst.

YOUR BREATHING EXERCISES

Expand your ribs to their fullest by walking erect all the time, breathing in and out deeply and rhythmically as you go. Shoulders back, head up. And, standing before an open window, breathe regularly and deeply, in through the nose, out through the mouth. Always keep your nose clean. When you cough it is because foreign matter has passed to your throat via your nose. Avoid spending long in hot places as far as you can. *Think* about your breathing—often. It is a function in life taken too much for granted. Make it an integral part of your life. Breathe as if you liked it. Think positive thoughts as you breathe in and out—regularly.

POSSIBLE PEAK AGE OF VIRILITY AND PHYSICAL PERFECTION

Late in life, but when it comes it will be good. That is not to say you will not be fit and well until there are many years behind you. It means that physical perfection will be at its most perfect and outstanding when your hair is greying and your purposeful personality has reached its zenith. With this will come added strength and vigour which will enable you to carry out many duties, to accomplish much more, than the average person of the same age group. Middle age should see a finely developed constitution, strength of body and mind. Keep your feeding habits sensible, drink little and watch smoking if you *do*. Lots of sleep will be necessary in earlier

adult years but you will be able to cut down as you grow
older.

PISCES—THE FISHES

Healthwise you go in many directions at the same time.
Under the weather at times, you keep going. Fit and well,
you feel a certain lassitude. You are virile, vigorous, versatile.
But you can be depressed, repressed, oppressed. Your con-
ception of optimum health is the ability to be up and doing
all of the time until the warning signs of nature make themselves felt. You shake off minor conditions of ill-health very
successfully. Weakest spot is the solar-plexus, seat of the
emotions, from which spring many functional disorders
entirely dictated by your mind.

ARIES
March 21—April 20

CONSTITUTION

Headaches are your chief béte noir. Migraine, mostly
functional, is likely to occur, if not now, possibly in later
life. But it can be controlled by strength of mind. Pay special
attention to your eyes. Visit the optician at the first signs of
trouble. Or if you already wear glasses, keep in touch for
frequent re-tests. Your eyes will be kept working hard
throughout your life.

DEFICIENCY MINERAL

KALI. PHOS. (Potassium Phosphate). This mineral
assists function of the nervous system, from which your headaches arise. Brain-fag is well helped by this mineral. Hard
study becomes far easier. Also consider NAT. SUR (Sodium
Chloride) which is good for the eyes.

ESSENTIAL VITAMIN-NEEDS

Vitamin A, to be found in butter, margarine, eggs, milk, liver oil. This vitamin is of special value as it brightens the eyes, gives lustre to the hair and keeps the skin clear. It will help to keep your vision clear—purify your blood stream. Depression rising from headaches will clear with a good intake of this valuable Vitamin A.

TRY THIS SPECIAL DIET

Poached egg, celery, carrots. Glass of milk.

YOUR BREATHING EXERCISES

Deep breathing—counting to five, in, out, in, out, in, out. Then step up counting to nine. Then increase again, counting to twelve. Do this each day for a week, starting with five, up to twelve, back to five, through nine to twelve. Breathe in—count to five, *expel*. In, count to nine—*expel*. In, count to twelve—*expel*. This will control the supply of oxygen to your brain—help to relieve those headaches. Particularly, try this when you feel a headache or a bout of migraine on its way.

POSSIBLE PEAK AGE OF VIRILITY AND PHYSICAL PERFECTION

Three decades of life is not much in a lifetime, but by the time you reach thirty you will have lived a great deal in terms of experience. That age should find you at your best, virile, strong and powerful. Intellectually, you will be well on your way to your zenith. Physically, you should possess optimum strength though your looks may belie this. The periodic headaches could well be on their way out if you have taken good care of yourself. If not, make thirty your starting-off age to self-cure. If you are now over thirty, and have not yet felt your whole strength, now will be the time to start to pull your socks up and *realise* your own strength.

ARIES—THE RAM

Healthwise you have dynamic drive. An innate force drives you forward. Dogged, you forge ahead, in spite of physical discomforts, those headaches and sometimes poor vision. You are the leader-type and your particular, wiry energy inspires others. You may put your head up against a brick wall from

time to time, but you do not let your constitution get the
better of you. Powers of endurance help you through many a
difficult period. Out of pain is brought forth inspiration for
future moves.

TAURUS
April 21—May 21

CONSTITUTION

Obesity will be your enemy, if it is not so now. But you
can offset this by developing sane eating habits. Reading
some of the diets given for Sun Sign subjects other than
yours will come in useful to help you beat approach of over-
fatness. Read them now, as well as the diet at the end of *this*
section. You may get fat because you are content, or because
you indulge your tastes for good food and luxuries too much.
Or because you give way to smugness and feel all's well with
your particular little world too often. You also have what is
called a 'nervous heart'. Do not be alarmed! This is far
more a functional (mind) complaint than anything else.
That means *you* can control it by right thinking and by not
dwelling too much on the possibilities of conditions of the
heart. Variations in your blood pressure must not give cause
for alarm, but if you eat wisely and allow yourself plenty of
rest and relaxation, you will be all set for a long life.

DEFICIENCY MINERAL

NAT. SULPH. (Sodium Sulphate). This mineral controls
retention of water in the system and will have a good effect
upon any 'fatty' tendencies you may develop.

ESSENTIAL VITAMIN-NEEDS

Vitamin A, to be found in butter, margarine, eggs, milk,
liver oil. And Vitamins C and D, in raw tomatoes, lemons,

oranges, vegetables, in lettuce, cod and halibut liver oils, eggs. These three vitamins will purify your blood stream, prevent sluggishness, strengthen your bones.

TRY THIS SPECIAL DIET

No white sugar, white bread. All-fruit diet for a week.

YOUR BREATHING EXERCISES

Inhale and exhale slowly through the nose, mouth tightly shut. After a short interval of ten minutes or so, do it again. And again. About six times in all. First thing in the morning and last thing at night are best times.

POSSIBLE PEAK AGE OF VIRILITY AND PHYSICAL PERFECTION

You will always be virile, perhaps a little too much so. This will be controlled, to a great degree, by your attitude to life. There will be times when your physical self seems to falter, due to the oppressiveness of the extra weight we have mentioned and the 'nervous' heart you may bring upon yourself by too fevered an imagination. All in all, however, you will be up to the usual standards of fitness, and although not able to pin-point any particular time of your life in which you can feel you *have* reached a climax of good health, you will be conscious of growing strength, and not particularly aware of the normal ebb in later years.

TAURUS—THE BULL

Healthwise you stand on hot bricks. Flabby, fluid but with great resistance. Strong nerved at times, possessed of a spirit that demands more of your body than the onlooker would think it could give. Slow in movement, yet vital at a moment's notice. A hidden dynamo lurks within you, supercharged. Your instincts are to blindly charge, sure of your objective and well aware of bodily-skill to carry you where you wish to go. You have a stubborn resistance, yet give way to weakness, looseness of limb, shortness of breath and become acutely aware of pain—mostly of your own imagining.

GEMINI
May 22—June 21

CONSTITUTION

You have a rather tender skin. Your complexion has to be well cared for, whether male or female. If this is a sensitive point with you, care and attention will soon remove the sources of blemishes and irritations. A relaxed throat attacks you upon occasion—especially in moments of stress. This is more a functional complaint than anything else and is 'escape' mechanism when you are worried. There is nothing at all wrong with you—but your weakest spot *is* your throat, to which negative mind-messages fly when trouble threatens. The psychology of this is to make you unable to speak—therefore you do not have to solve your immediate problems. Face up to life a bit more—and this will disappear. The same obtains with any skin complaints. You probably suffer from a 'nervous' rash due to an over-heated bloodstream due to anxiety thoughts. At the same time, you are prone to have stomach 'flutters' which you ascribe to flatulence. In reality, this is the result of the nerves of your solar plexus reacting to negative worry thoughts. It would seem you are a highly-strung, tensed-up person, though you may well not realise this.

DEFICIENCY MINERAL

CAL. SULPH. (Calcium Sulphate). This mineral, used with KALI. MUR (Potassium Chloride) is excellent for treating acne, skin eruptions and so on. It has, in conjunction with KALI. MUR, a cooling effect upon the blood stream. It is also excellent for sore and relaxed throats, and removes impurities from the bloodstream, so improving digestive functions.

ESSENTIAL VITAMIN-NEEDS

Vitamin B$_2$, to be found in fish, milk, eggs, cereals, vegetables.

TRY THIS SPECIAL DIET

A week on an all-fruit diet, no starchy foods. Drink pure fruit juices. No white sugar. No condiments with salads. No white bread. Take wholemeal toast.

YOUR BREATHING EXERCISES

Long daily sessions of breathing full and deep in the open air, preferably away from town—if this is possible. Otherwise, in front of an open window first thing each morning. On summer nights, before you go to bed.

POSSIBLE PEAK AGE OF VIRILITY AND PHYSICAL PERFECTION

Looking back on your Psycho-Sign we see that your Peak Age of Power may never be reached as you will experience many little peaks. Nevertheless, you will be always strong and virile. In spite of the 'nerves' in your stomach and your way of reacting to stress, you will forever be keyed up to concert pitch. Because of this, you will always be on the alert, and, like the highly-strung mechanism you are, you will achieve more than a great deal as far as physical output is concerned. Always you will give the impression of being stronger than you actually are. At the age of fifty, as your Psycho-Sign shows, you may well reach your zenith of power which will also mean your peak of perfection in health. This may be the case instead of reaching those smaller, more scattered peaks. It is greatly in the balance all round but rest assured you are not likely to develop into a weak, negative—*physical* personality.

GEMINI—THE TWINS

Healthwise you are two people. Strong within and seemingly, at times, weak. But you have the laugh on others because you possess a twin physical personality. Great joy and deep depression alternate to make you a flexible, physical organism.

CANCER
June 22—July 23

CONSTITUTION
Pretty good, but for a tendency to hurry meals which gives you gastritis from time to time. Nothing specially serious.

DEFICIENCY MINERAL
SILICA. (Silicic Oxide). This mineral helps elimination. It strengthens your nerves. Dyspepsia reacts favourably to this mineral. An active, clear skin is achieved.

ESSENTIAL VITAMIN-NEEDS
Vitamin E, to be found in lettuce, wheat germ, whole grain cereals, eggs. This vitamin helps your muscle development and your reproductory powers. This is the 'virility' vitamin. It fights stress, strain, fatigue, debility—tendencies you possess and which give rise to gastric conditions.

TRY THIS SPECIAL DIET
Vegetables, consisting of onions, turnips, celery, cucumber, tomatoes. Cut down on starchy foods such as potatoes. Add to your proteins with nuts, lentils, beans. Pears and oranges will be good for you, also raisins and figs. Try a short fast for a day or two, living mostly on fruit juices. It *can* be done! Keep away from tea for a while. If your social life demands aperitifs, short drinks, cocktails, cut down on them quite often. This way, you will aid cure of your gastric tendencies. You are the sort of person who should never eat when tired or overwrought. Your stomach muscles just cannot cope with the business of digesting food when you have been under a strain. And don't eat when you are tired —either. Try to reach a sense of balance where your eating habits are concerned.

YOUR BREATHING EXERCISES

Your physique will improve with good, hard breathing exercises. If male, you must check a tendency, now, or later, to develop a 'paunch'. Lazy living may bring this on you. If female, preserve your figure with regular, planned breathing exercises. Deep breathing to a count of five after you have breathed in, up to a count of nine, then to twelve as you improve, is advisable. You need to get really good, clean fresh air from the country. Combine this with plenty of good hard exercise from time to time.

POSSIBLE PEAK AGE OF VIRILITY AND PHYSICAL PERFECTION

Because of your rather immature outlook, you are apt to put physical comforts before commonsense bodily functions and development. This predilection for warmth, comfort and the easy way out of hardship tends to make you flabby. You are likely, therefore, to miss-out on a peak age as shown in your Psycho-Sign. Virile—you may be, and up to scratch when you wish, but you feel pretty exhausted after serious physical effort—whenever you go in for it.

CANCER—THE CRAB

Healthwise you are an enigma. Your looks don't tell when you are ill any more than feeling ill makes you look unwell. You are a source of worry to those who love you, not because you are ever likely to be an invalid but because you play ducks and drakes with your constitution to the dismay of those around you. You could be described as an 'actor-hypochondriac' insomuch as you have the knack of switching on 'ailments' at will—to suit the occasion or circumstance. Rock-bottom, you are as fit as the rest apart from the gastric troubles which arise mainly from your attitude to life and your love of getting sympathy from unsuspecting or sorely-tried associates.

LEO
July 24—August 23

CONSTITUTION

There may be bronchial tendencies, mostly of nervous origin, therefore not serious. You need to readjust your outlook on life, not to be so anxiety-ridden, and this trouble could soon clear up. You may also suffer from 'nervous heart', a truly functional complaint due, in the main, to your indecisive habits, your ability to side-step responsibilities which give occasion for acute anxiety from time to time. Realise that physically, you are no doubt very fit. It is your mind, sending negative messages to your body that makes your constitution appear a bit 'delicate'.

DEFICIENCY MINERAL

KALI. PHOS. (Potassium Phosphate). This mineral is for the nerves. It aids the nervous system to function coolly and calmly. Also. KALI. SULPH. (Potassium Sulphate) for respiration and the relief of catarrhal conditions.

ESSENTIAL VITAMIN-NEEDS

Vitamin B_1, to be found in fish, milk, eggs, cereals, vegetables. This vitamin steadies the nerves, helps in times of stress.

TRY THIS SPECIAL DIET

A week on protein-intake—from eggs, cheese, fish, nuts, peas, poultry, beans. Herrings will be good too. Onions are not to be sniffed at, and have cereals to start each day. Include lentils for lunch.

YOUR BREATHING EXERCISES

Deep breathing to compensate for anxiety-thoughts. When worry sets in, breathe calmly, slowly, evenly. Develop rhythmic breathing. This will clear your bronchial tubes, help you to make decisions in a calm state of mind. Every day, at the window, before the day's work starts.

POSSIBLE PEAK AGE OF VIRILITY AND PHYSICAL PERFECTION

Since you seek peace of mind, in spite of your way of worrying over so many things, it is highly probable you will find this round about middle age, and this will mean your health in general will have settled down well by then. You will feel strong and virile on many occasions throughout your life, but more so when you have reached the late forties and early fifties. You have always had a certain inward peace of mind though this is ruined from time to time by your anxiety-thoughts. A sense of humour will bubble to the surface from time to time and, no doubt, will be your ultimate saving grace. A lot of people will be made very happy by a sudden and apparently miraculous recovery you will make in your spirits and enjoyment of life. This of course will be followed by a great change for the good in your health.

LEO—THE LION

Healthwise, you are a bundle of electricity. Looked upon as leaders, but sometimes the *led*, Leo subjects have reserves of energy that they will only let loose upon the world when they are completely free from worry and the path is clear in front of them. Vitality springs forth from time to time, and, when it does, tremendous impact is made. You can switch your well-being and physical peak on and off at will, as the moods take you. You are a considerable source of worry to others because of your apparently elusive energy. But you know it is there and ready to be used when you permit it to be.

VIRGO
August 24—September 23

CONSTITUTION

Due to your inner drive, you have a 'fluttering' stomach and crises go straight there. You will grow out of this if you are young. If you are getting on in years—it will be advisable to pull yourself together and to stop allowing things to get you down. Also, your fluttery stomach arises from your sometimes extraordinary way of working yourself up into a fever-pitch of excitement over matters in hand. You are also subject to occasional moods of depression. These have an immediate effect on your head—giving you unnecessary headaches and eye-strain. You have strong eyes, but tend to weaken the nervous system controlling them by this deliberate habit of over-anxiety. An introspective nature doesn't help matters, either. Basically—you are a strong person, virile and active, but you sap your physical strength by using up far too much adrenalin—far too often.

DEFICIENCY MINERAL

KALI. PHOS. (Potassium Phosphate). This mineral will work wonders for your nervous system. It will calm you down. NAT. PHOS. (Sodium Phosphate). The neutraliser mineral that assists proper functioning of your system of digestion.

ESSENTIAL VITAMIN-NEEDS

Vitamin B_1, to be found in vegetables, nuts, fruit, cereals. This vitamin is good for frayed nerves, but its principle function is to help lactation, give you a good appetite and generally to help you digest your meals better. Excellent for that 'nervous' stomach.

TRY THIS SPECIAL DIET

Grapefruits, raw vegetable salads. Wholemeal bread and butter. Milk. Fresh fruit salads.

YOUR BREATHING EXERCISES

For you especially—deep, rhythmic, controlled breathing, to help you control your emotions, especially when you feel yourself likely to fly off at a tangent. Try breathing in and out to the count of five, stepping up to nine, then to twelve. A week or two of this would make all the difference to your temperament.

POSSIBLE PEAK AGE OF VIRILITY AND PHYSICAL PERFECTION

You will burn up quickly, the flame will die down from time to time and then you will be ready for another peak-period. That is a good picture of your physical self. But, like all fires that are difficult to control, you will go on burning for a very long time. Possibly when you are approaching middle age, you will reach your flash-point, and remain steady for many years after. A tiny little spiritual 'flame' burns steadily in the background. This is your saving grace. It is the ability to recognise and to sympathise with the ills of others. This is the subduing factor that will help you to keep on top of yourself, will prevent your burning up too much fuel too quickly.

VIRGO—THE VIRGIN

Healthwise, you are cautious over matters to do with your body while at the same time, utterly careless with the way in which you allow your mind to control your physical self. A desire for a high standard of morals will keep you from excesses that might otherwise prove injurious.

LIBRA
September 24—October 23

CONSTITUTION
Kidney troubles may cause a little concern but these will,

in the main, be superficial, responding easily to treatment should occasion arise. There may also be a history of rheumatic troubles, in the main when the weather is on the turn, and not based on deep-rooted constitutional causes.

DEFICIENCY MINERAL

NAT. SULPH. (Sodium Sulphate). This mineral helps elimination of water in excess of the body's requirements. The kidneys play an important role in this process of elimination. Also NAT. PHOS. (Sodium Phosphate), for the rheumatic tendencies. This mineral adjusts acidity of the bloodstream and contributes towards relief of rheumatics.

ESSENTIAL VITAMIN-NEEDS

Vitamin B_2 to assist in clearing the bloodstream of impurities. Also to help the gastric juices to correctly function. Vitamin C also, for this vitamin strengthens the bones as well as the teeth, gums and the skin. Rheumatic conditions will respond well to this vitamin.

TRY THIS SPECIAL DIET

Get more protein from cheese and eggs of which you should consume a great deal per month. Keep off tea and coffee for, say, a week, and make up with pure fruit juices. Cocoa should also be avoided. Apples and grapes will fill you and do you no end of good. A spread of the Marmite variety will be good on wholemeal bread. Avoid all starchy foods. You might like to try buttermilk, too.

YOUR BREATHING EXERCISES

Expanding your stomach muscles by breathing slowly in and out will be good for you. Stand erect before an open window and make your breathing slow, regular and rhythmical. A measured count of three, going up to five to begin with is advisable. Later step it up to nine and then to twelve. This will improve all-round circulation of the bloodstream and keep the water waste-matters in your body flowing regularly. Rheumatic crystals will have less of an easy task to form where they give the most discomfort.

POSSIBLE PEAK AGE OF VIRILITY AND PHYSICAL PERFECTION

Up and down, one-hundred per-cent today, a bit under

the weather tomorrow. But a general picture of good health and you will certainly spend most of your life being extremely virile. You will, from time to time, tend to overwork your body at your physical and mental jobs. Powers of recuperation, however, will be strong. Yours will be a history of a wavy line for many years until a point is reached when satisfactory health, (mental and physical) sets in, to be enjoyed for many a year. Beware, though, of that inviting candle that can be burnt at both ends.

LIBRA—THE SCALES

Healthwise, you are the up-and-down type, just like the scales, but give a fair measure throughout life. Your mental output is considerable. You are mercurial in thought, elusive where looks are concerned, for they belie your health. One moment serene, placid to the point of cussedness, the next, up in the air, overwrought, high-temperatured. Electric but forceful, your health is the topic of conversation with your associates, who, in turn, despair of it and envy it.

SCORPIO
October 24—November 22

CONSTITUTION

You are another sufferer from 'nervous' stomach. There are so many people in the world afflicted with this rather unnecessary complaint. Due, in the main, to their way of life and their attitude to it. Pulling your socks up will help you get over this condition. You spoil enjoyment of your meals by upsetting gastric juices by over-worry. Try to settle your problems (if you must *have* problems) before you sit down at mealtimes. It will make all the difference to you. Also, try to calm down when faced with a crisis. It goes straight to your stomach. Lumbago is another of your little trials in life—or *may* be—later on.

DEFICIENCY MINERAL

CAL. FLUOR. (Calcium Fluoride). This mineral is ideal for treatment of inflamed joints and 'tired' bones. It will be good for you when you have twitches of lumbago. As for the 'nervous' stomach—try KALI. PHOS. (Potassium Phosphate). This mineral will calm the flutters, make you a more reasoned thinker, slow-up your panic-processes. Nervous indigestion responds favourably to this mineral.

ESSENTIAL VITAMIN-NEEDS

Vitamin B_1 for you, to help your digestive process work to order, to help that stomach cope with the extra work it has to do to because you eat with a plateful of anxiety on your menu. Try Vitamin C, too, the vitamin the body cannot store. Find B_1 in nuts, fruits, cereals and vegetables, and C in raw tomatoes, lemons, oranges and also in vegetables.

TRY THIS SPECIAL DIET

An all-fruit diet would go down well in more ways than one if you could manage it for a week. You might also be able to worry quite well at the same time—*and* also feed yourself well!

YOUR BREATHING EXERCISES

Lifting the abdomen will be good for you. Clasp the hands behind the back standing very straight. Using the best muscular power you can call forth—pull in the lower abdomen and then upwards to the chest. Keep this hold for as long as you are able, then let the abdomen sag and relax. Do this until you begin to feel pleasantly tired. Then lie on your back and lift your legs, taking care to keep them straight and rigid. Try to hold them at forty-five degrees for a short while, then lower them slowly. Without subjecting yourself to undue strain—do these exercises until you have to admit you really *do* feel tired.

POSSIBLE PEAK AGE OF VIRILITY AND PHYSICAL PERFECTION

The fighter-type, naturally your stomach suffers. This

could well retard your complete health-picture for quite a few years until you are able to settle down into a more balanced person. You will be virile more or less most of the time after you have passed the middle 'teens since you will be living at a great pace.

SCORPIO—THE SCORPION

Healthwise, misunderstood and wrongly diagnosed—most of the while. People will not be able to understand. But will envy you your great resistance to real, genuine ills. You are ruthless in your determination to refute illness—despite various little inner qualms you may hug to yourself from time to time.

SAGITTARIUS
November 23—December 22

CONSTITUTION

Your limbs are likely to play you up from time to time. Rheumatism will be your main bug-bear. But this will be easy to control for it will never really get a hold on you. You are the nervous type. There are many of them. Few escape, in these days of hectic 'here and there' in a few seconds or so.

DEFICIENCY MINERAL

Kali. Sulph. (Potassium Sulphate). This mineral helps you overcome feelings of being hemmed-in, makes you generally more agile, assists the normal flow of the blood-stream. It will also help your limbs and joints to ease up, because it will greatly assist 'lubrication'.

TRY THIS SPECIAL DIET

Keep close to raw vegetables from time to time. Vitamins come to you direct from the sun. You can get more than a fair share of inner sunshine by eating plenty of green things, and supplementing daily foods with fruit and fruit juices. A starch-content is found in potatoes. Have more than your normal supply every other week, say, for a month.

YOUR BREATHING EXERCISES

Do not let a morning go by without deep-breathing exercises in front of an open window. Take plenty of exercise in your spare time, especially at weekends. Breathe deeply when walking, head erect, chest out. Get yourself used to rhythmic breathing which you can practise from time to time when no one is watching.

POSSIBLE PEAK AGE OF VIRILITY AND PHYSICAL PERFECTION

Good health will grow on you, slowly at first. But later in life, probably when it really matters, you will find yourself virile, vigorous and full of vitality. Mentally, you will be most alert at middle age, though, at various times throughout your life, you will feel a great inner mental and physical power and strength rising in you. This will have a tendency to ebb and flow. Do not be discouraged when sometimes you feel extra low and dispirited. This will only be a 'rest' period during which your body is gathering impetus for a fresh, vital assault on life's problems.

SAGITTARIUS—THE ARCHER

Healthwise, you go straight to the point when you have made a certain physical aim your main ambition. You are a straight dealer, but fond of journeys into unexplored territories. You have the physical make-up that will see you through many hard tests of endurance.

THE STARS PASS ON TO YOUR PERSONAL 'AURA'

The Stars have shown you how weak you are, how strong you are. You have a good idea—now—of exactly the sort of person you are. You have found out a lot about your friends you did not know about before.

Now, you are going to pass from the mental which you have explored, through the physical you have just finished learning about—to the sort of personality you possess as far as your 'aura' is concerned.

Your 'aura' is that indefinable something that surrounds you wherever you go, that decides whether or not people are going to like you.

Everyone has his or her own, individual 'aura'. Call it spiritual personality. Call it your vibrations. But whatever you choose to call it—it is with you throughout your life. You react to it in other people. Wonder why you get on so very well with old So-and-So, hate the other So-and-So.

And other people are aware of it in you also. That is why you succeed in this job, fail in that. Make your mark in that social sphere—fail to make any impression whatsoever in the other. Your personal Star 'aura' can help you on in life. It is responsible for the things that push you forward. Can be blamed for the things that hold you back.

Bear in mind that your mental and physical self *and* your Star 'aura' have everything in the world in common. Your Mind-Self, your Body-Self and your Personality-Self are bound together by your personal 'aura'.

After your Star 'aura' you will learn about your Star Make-Up, then will follow the more material things—the stones, metals, lucky numbers and days, that go to complete the Star picture of you and your life.

Now continue your studies.

PART THREE

Your Star-Aura

Individual Guidance to your positive and negative 'drives' and 'influences' in life. Your love life and emotional outlets.

YOUR STAR-AURA

CAPRICORN
December 23—January 20

YOUR SENSE OF HUMOUR

Apt to be rather laboured at times, due to your serious outlook on life. You feel you have something to which to live up to and this robs you of the ability to take a joke against yourself. Smarten up your ideas and get a more sophisticated outlook on life.

YOUR POSITIVE 'SUCCESS DRIVE'

This lies in your ability to work very hard. Determination will get you what you want. This is your biggest success factor for the future.

YOUR NEGATIVE 'PULL-BACK'

Is the way in which you look down at yourself and fail, at times, to make the most of your abilities. This could be the biggest factor to contribute to any personal failures in life.

YOUR LOVE LIFE

Your desire to do things for others will, one day, win you a partner ready to reflect your acts of kindness and give you the appreciation you long for. If you have, by now, found that partner in life, you can look forward to a long period of great happiness. But be careful not to let yourself down in the eyes of your partner or partner-to-be. Your sense of loyalty will need a partner with an equal sense of comradeship. You will love very passionately and your union will be lasting. You will find intellectual companionship taking precedence over your emotional life in the long run. This will be successful, as your intelligence will have more demands to make than will your physical self. Your love life will contain a great deal of ups and downs but, all in all, will prove to be most satisfactory.

AQUARIUS
January 21—February 19

YOUR SENSE OF HUMOUR

Being a sensitive person, this is not very highly developed. You cannot grasp the subtleties of smart humour, preferring the 'slapstick' to the more elusive type of humour.

YOUR POSITIVE 'SUCCESS DRIVE'

Your uncanny insight into other people's motive and potential moves. Make the most of this gift. It is likely to lead you on rapidly. A fluent speaker, you should also utilise your power of persuasion to greatest advantage.

YOUR NEGATIVE 'PULL-BACK'

The biggest failure-factor in your life could be the way in which you are easily hurt and have sometimes a fixed idea people are against you. Your desire to make sacrifices for others will not always be wise, as there will be someone ready to take advantage of you.

YOUR LOVE LIFE

Your partner in life is—or will be—a person who will lean on you in times of trouble. Who will take strength from you. A person who will share your love for children. You will always be emotionally fulfilled. There will be little friction in your married life in later years, due to your ability to adapt yourself to circumstances and to accept the ideas of others even if they do not always fit in with your own. Certain physical fears in your life will win you a partner with a highly developed instinct for protecting you—if you have not already found this to be true now. Generally your love life will be a placid affair. Heights of emotionalism will not be reached but you will get the very most out of it according to your rather mixed-up temperament.

PISCES
February 20—March 20

YOUR SENSE OF HUMOUR

Is light-hearted, gay at times. Tends to be whimsical. Fantasies you love, especially if connected with others.

YOUR POSITIVE 'SUCCESS DRIVE'

Your great sense of values and of hard cash. Use this to best advantage when negotiating important money deals. You can foresee—this makes you 'canny'. People love this, while it may dismay them a little.

YOUR NEGATIVE 'PULL-BACK'

Could well be your desire to mix with more simple types. You fear, to a certain extent, sophisticated surroundings and groups of people with whom you feel you will be a fish out of water. Think more of yourself—try to project your personality far more than you do

YOUR LOVE LIFE

Your simple outlook on life, when you are not driving a hard bargain and being materialistic leads you into the company of unsophisticates. From them you will draw quite a few partners—outside the bonds of marriage. With them you will find emotional satisfaction and an outlet for sometimes frustrated feelings. A mean trait in you will win disfavour from someone you specially love. Beware of letting this tendency overrule you. If married, you will cleave to your partner, and should enjoy the same degree of loyalty. If single, you will pass through many stages of unrest before you finally settle down. The overall picture is one of emotional fulfilment from an early age, but only because you will change partners a great deal until you finally become settled. There may be a few people who, under the guise of love and affection, will seek to take advantage of certain weakness in your character. Apart from that, there will be many loyal ones ready to stand by you through thick and thin. Let your hair down more than you are used to doing. Go out for adventure in your love life. If married, be a bit more venturesome with your partner. Added happiness will be your reward in both cases.

ARIES
March 21—April 20

YOUR SENSE OF HUMOUR

Artificial—and people are never quite sure how to take you. You enjoy a joke against others but are not too happy when the joke is on *you*.

YOUR POSITIVE 'SUCCESS DRIVE'

Organising ability, the power to dominate, an ability to command. But an overbearing manner must be carefully watched.

YOUR NEGATIVE 'PULL-BACK'

Anticipation of crisis and mild panic when it happens. This will land you in hot water many times.

YOUR LOVE LIFE

Because you love to flirt you will hurt a lot of people of your opposite sex. It may be a time before you are serious enough and responsible enough to marry. If now married, you will have to control your flirtatious, capricious nature. It will not be an easy job to persuade the right one you are genuinely sincere. And, if already married, you will have times ahead in which you will have to win your partner all over again. Your emotions do not go very deep, though they may change as you get older and wiser. There will be one or two smart members of your opposite sex who will turn you down on the grounds of your lackadaisical manners and lack of dress-sense. You take people too much for granted sometimes. This robs you of absolute fulfilment, most of the time. You are not fully mature emotionally and have a tendency to cling on to the past when you were happy as a child. You will have to learn to discriminate between adult love and that undeveloped emotionalism that belongs more to the cradle than to the modern family scene.

TAURUS
April 21—May 21

YOUR SENSE OF HUMOUR

Is of the sympathetic variety. You will laugh with others to support them and to give them courage. You take a good joke against yourself. Your humour is kind, neither cynical nor biting.

YOUR 'POSITIVE SUCCESS DRIVE'

Great courage, both physical and mental. Your powers of intuition. Your tolerance.

YOUR NEGATIVE 'PULL-BACK'

Your spendthrift nature. You love luxury too much. Reluctant to delve deep, you are likely to fail in things that matter. The surface is always good enough. You also have the ability, if it can be called that, to put people off you because you so quickly and readily become biased.

YOUR LOVE LIFE

May be very erratic because you expect to dominate your partner—or partners. If married you will find this unwork-able. If unattached, it will be the main obstacle to emotional happiness. Lacking tenderness, you cannot see the loved-one's point of view, or cater for your close companion's immediate and most intimate wishes and desires. On the good side, you will quite likely find ultimate fulfilment of body and soul once you either meet someone who admires your courage first and foremost, or, in a married state, are able to let your fearlessness override all other considerations in the eyes of the one who loves you. You may easily make someone a most exciting partner, young in heart, young in body, virile and venturesome. But that person may take some time to discover. Or, if you are married, it may take a long time to get your partner to share your somewhat bizarre outlook and way of life. But persevere. Many in history have been just like you and have, in the end, been completely fulfilled, emotionally and physically.

GEMINI
May 22—June 21

YOUR SENSE OF HUMOUR

Your changeable moods prevent your having a well developed sense of fun. Too intense, you fail to see the lighter side of life. But this may improve as time goes on.

YOUR POSITIVE 'SUCCESS DRIVE'

Faith in Providence and in yourself is the greatest factor in your life. Your unselfish nature will take you far.

YOUR NEGATIVE 'PULL-BACK'

Stop hurting yourself. You will end up by putting so many people against you. This is your biggest failing. Cut it out of your life and success could come more quickly than you think.

YOUR LOVE LIFE

Will be staid. Perhaps even a little bit prim. But if you meet the right partner, or already have done—there are hopes of a happy, rather 'old-fashioned' relationship being enjoyed over a prolonged period. Don't look forward to, or try to manufacture, an exciting relationship with a loved one. The glamour's not for you. Possibly all to the good. You are the sort of person to appreciate solidity and genuineness. A highly intellectual union may well be formed or develop out of a present relationship in which you are involved. On the other hand, you may prefer an emotional outlet that will satisfy the physical side of your life while leaving you to enjoy the spiritual and philosophical aspects of existence on your own. Beware of trying to analyse and dissect the human relationship too much. It is not everyone who is critical by nature, and not everyone can understand or accept the search for perfection. Be happy with what you get—or with what you already have—sure and certain that destiny knows what it is doing for you all along the line.

CANCER
June 22—July 23

YOUR SENSE OF HUMOUR

Could be a rather coarse, secret sense of humour. Provided you keep this to yourself—all's well and good. A pity, though, for underneath its broadness, your outlook on the lighter side of life could well be adapted to make you popular with others. Try getting a bit outside of yourself.

YOUR POSITIVE 'SUCCESS-DRIVE'

Will lie in your strength of will and ability to divine forward moves. Also in the way in which you can, if you wish, be most ingenious with your hands.

YOUR NEGATIVE 'PULL-BACK'

Meanness with money and the way in which you are unwilling, at times, to open up and mix with your contemporaries.

YOUR LOVE LIFE

Could well be something very special, on the lines of a 'grand passion'. But only once in your life. Either to come in the foreseeable future, or at this very moment. You are the sort of person who is extremely sparing with affections, though capable of giving a great deal—once roused. If you are still young you will find experimentation with love distasteful. Middle-aged—and it will occupy a great deal of your time in a subtle, refined fashion. Getting on past middle age—and you may yet have a great deal to which to look forward emotionally. Your outlook on love and close personal relationships has as its roots a close alliance with your parents. Analysis of your own love life will therefore largely be based on childhood impressions. Your first real emotional experience will have stayed with you, deeply impressed on your mind.

LEO
July 24—August 23

YOUR SENSE OF HUMOUR

Free and easy, indolent, carefree. You could be great fun in company.

YOUR POSITIVE 'SUCCESS-DRIVE'

Inborn sense of domesticity. Your home-loving tendencies will help you make a success of your domestic and home life. As far as work is concerned—your devil-may-care outlook could take you far. Not because of any particular skill, but because people will like having you around. You could be an asset to many an organisation merely from a prestige point of view. There may not be much money in that—however. But you will find happiness.

YOUR NEGATIVE 'PULL-BACK'

Laziness of mind, dislike of physical effort could set you back. Your personality may override all this. But watch it. You may not always get away with it.

YOUR LOVE LIFE

Someone will be inspired to love you and to share your happy-go-lucky existence. If not now—later. If already married, the day will come (if not now) when your partner will suddenly adapt to your particular and individual outlook. Emotionally, you are full of 'give'. Uninhibited, unfrustrated. You may have some difficulty for a while in getting a close partner to be quite so free as you are. Generally, and all round, a happy picture of eventual happiness in love. You are quite likely to marry someone older by quite a few years—if you have not already done so. This applies to both sexes. Domestic harmony will be enjoyed in bohemian surroundings where a strong sense of domesticity is apparent but hidden under the guise of attractive untidiness.

VIRGO
August 24—September 23

YOUR SENSE OF HUMOUR

Not fully developed because you are too particular about too many things. A precise nature holds you back and keeps a real sense of fun out of your life.

YOUR POSITIVE 'SUCCESS DRIVE'

Your attention to detail. But do not let this get an obsession or a compulsion with you. Perfectionism can be damaging sometimes. Your sense of responsibility, highly developed as it is, should win you an executive position now—or later in life.

YOUR NEGATIVE 'PULL-BACK'

Getting there quickly instead of plodding gamely on might make you miss-out many times. Your tendency to be self-opinionated is no asset, either.

YOUR LOVE LIFE

Could well be influenced in your favour because of your latent psychic powers. Possibly you will meet up with someone of similar gifts. Together, you could reach great emotional heights. That ultimate happiness is in store—even if it has not yet been achieved—is for sure. You may well find, in your love life, new and untried ways of emotional and spiritual bliss. It may be that the way in which you are able to soothe others in trouble could lead to complications. Many may be after your favours. But you will, all the time—be aware of a great shining light ahead of you. And this will be your ultimate goal. Possibly—you have already attained that goal. If so—you will find happiness will begin to grow far greater as the years roll by. At least once—you will be responsible for a great triumph of healing in some way or the other and this will win you great affection amounting almost to devotion from your partner.

LIBRA
September 24—October 23

YOUR SENSE OF HUMOUR

You take your cue from others. You can laugh easily with

them, until someone says something with a sting in it. Then you are apt to quickly get hurt.

YOUR POSITIVE 'SUCCESS DRIVE'

Unbounded ambition and pretty good ability in your chosen activities or vocation will see you through eventually. Powers of concentration and great continuity of mind when you have to apply these qualities could guarantee success for you.

YOUR NEGATIVE 'PULL-BACK'

Taking too many risks and chances in life, using others to further your own ends are all negative tendencies that will need more than careful watching.

YOUR LOVE LIFE

Quite spectacular. You have unbounded enthusiasm for making conquests. This could apply even if you have settled down to married life already. If not, the way ahead will be strewn with opportunities to exert your personality and sex-appeal on members of your opposite sex. You will not always be an emotional adventurer—however. There will come a time when you are ready to pull in your horses and come down to earth—for keeps. Partners will find you exacting, very demanding and will have quite a time of it keeping up with your demands. Emotionally you will find perfect fulfilment, for you will be able to bend your companion's nature to your way of life. A partner with a similar outlook to yours would be the best choice.

SCORPIO
October 24—November 22

YOUR SENSE OF HUMOUR

Forced. Artificial. Try to cultivate a little genuineness.

Then people may find you an attractive person socially. Your humour is hardly subtle enough.

YOUR POSITIVE 'SUCCESS DRIVE'

Your ability to deny the existence of the word 'failure'. Your great desire to keep fit all of the time. Your go-ahead attitude to life.

YOUR NEGATIVE 'PULL-BACK'

The way flattery plays upon your vanity. The way in which you flaunt yourself and try to play life twice the size it really is.

YOUR LOVE LIFE

The person who marries you (or has already married you) will have to be strong-minded to withstand your assault upon their susceptibilities. Will have to be able to stand up to your emotional storms. Will you find that partner, or will you find happiness with a present partner? It is very much up to you alone. A fighter all of the way, you will also have to temper temperament with consideration for the feelings of your loved one. You are capable of reaching great heights in the love game. But you are in danger of dragging down the loved-one into a morass of false emotionalism or exaggerated sensationalism. Curb your instincts. Allow a few inhibitions to creep in. You must not go full blast all of the way all of the time. Your partner may not have the same powers of endurance you possess.

SAGITTARIUS
November 23—December 22

YOUR SENSE OF HUMOUR

Subject to fits and starts in which you can be capable of great wit. But those moments are few and far between.

YOUR POSITIVE 'SUCCESS DRIVE'

Ability to handle money—for others. Make the most of this. Accountancy might call if you put your mind to it. A job on the Stock Exchange could pay off. Try something like that.

YOUR NEGATIVE 'PULL-BACK'

Keeping things too much to yourself is not a wise thing to do. Share things more with others. And you have rather a one-track mind where it comes to business dealings. This stands you in good stead from a managerial point of view but does not contribute a great deal to your overall success in life.

YOUR LOVE LIFE

You will make out well with a domesticated partner. This façet of your personality will make plenty of people fond of you. If already married you should be pretty happy. If not, your emotional life should be fulfilled by meeting up with a person who is home-loving, tender and sympathetic. Your greatest happiness will lie in possessing a partner who will look up to you, mentally, physically and spiritually. If married now, you will have to train your chosen one along these lines. If single—make a serious attempt to be more than discriminating in making your final choice. You are the sort of person who will never be able to look back and make amends for mistakes made now—or in the past.

THE STARS PASS ON TO YOUR PERSONAL 'MAKE-UP'

Now you know what your personal 'aura' is like. That indefinable 'atmosphere' that surrounds you and governs your sense of humour, your positive drive and your negative 'pull-back'. Your personal 'aura' will be that invisible influence to which the one who is to love you *last* in life will react. Your personal 'aura' will accompany you throughout life—a powerful influence determining your life's destiny. Your Star has determined your 'aura'. No-one can change it.

Only *you* can use its positive and negative elements to good or bad effect.

You now begin to study, in the next part—Your Personal Star Make-up—the type of person you are (or should be) facially and physically. If you do not quite recognise your facial and physical characteristics, be sure the elements *are* there, either in bone structure, complexion, colour of hair or general build. And remember that, as the years pass, your face and physique alters. Experience leaves its mark on you. You will recognise your friends, may be able to visualise them as they will probably look—years ahead. Take particular care to note that special part of your face or body that needs most careful attention. So many people neglect their teeth or their hair, or let their figure go to seed through abject carelessness. By letting themselves go to pieces. Tell your friends and those in your family also—what *they* should do to preserve their dominant good features—so that they should not age, in appearance—too soon. Do the same for yourself. Do not pass over the tips on your dress sense. Clothes, style, ability to dress well—all these are priceless slants on the job of successful and happy living. Heed them as well.

Before you read on, note the following facts about the Twelve Signs of the Zodiac so that you should realise, and accept, why they are such potent forces in the lives of every human being put on earth.

The Twelve Signs of the Zodiac could be the framework upon which is built the structure called Man. Think of yourself as a vibration on earth, subject to the influences of the planetary powers from the moment of birth. The Prophets of the Old Testament accepted these influences. From ancient Babylon and Egypt came the science of the Stars. The Orientals made a great study of planetary influences. Europe in the Middle Ages worked by the stars until interest flagged. It was to be about three hundred years later that the Stars were once again to be accepted as vital influences in the passing of the decades, the deciding factors in wars, politics, religious beliefs.

Belief in the science of the Stars has increased as the years have gone by. The Twelve Signs of the Zodiac are now accepted by millions of people the world over as decisive factors in the destiny of the individual—of Mankind in general.

Modern usage of the language of the stars has, as its origin, writings from the Chaldeans, the Arabic, Latin and the sayings of the Greeks.

Today, there is hardly a popular newspaper or mass-circulation magazine without its astrological feature. These forecasts, because of limitations on space, naturally skim the surface and, in a few short paragraphs, give only a small idea of possibilities for the immediate future.

Probably you did not realise there *were* so many factors in your life coming under the influence of your particular star? It is not merely a question of what might happen *tomorrow*. It is more a question of continual influences for ever at work, controlling our destiny.

There are more important aspects of astrology than mere prediction—and those aspects you are studying in this book. That your psychological attitude to life is all-important is without question. In matters of health, mineral-therapy is all important as well. Vitamin-intake forms a vital part of the healthy, long life. Herbal-therapy is a useful sideline towards attainment and maintenance of good health, so the herbal indications supplied in Part Five are useful adjuncts.

The more material—and more popularly promoted aspects—such as lucky numbers, stones, metals, colours have their place in the visible interpretation of planetary influences. These you will learn in the final section of this book —Your Star Sign.

Take up your reading again, now, and discover even more interesting facts about yourself, your family and your friends.

PART FOUR

Your Personal Star 'Make-Up'

Individual indications of facial and physical appearance, advice on what particular physical weakness to strengthen and hints on your Dress-sense.

CAPRICORN
December 23—January 20

DOMINANT FACIAL CHARACTERISTICS
Tending to a pale complexion. Thin, sharp features. Well shaped nose—delicate nostrils. Hair—none too thick, but long-lasting. Deep-set eyes, rather thin lips.

DOMINANT PHYSICAL CHARACTERISTICS
Tall, thin. Large bones. Athletic. Likely to get fatter towards the middle years.

LOOK AFTER YOUR . . .
teeth. These are a good feature, but without regular attention, may be lost at an earlier age than is necessary.

YOUR DRESS SENSE
Not very well developed. You tend to be behind the times. Get more sophistication into your choice of colours.

MEN. Break out a bit more. Try to be less conservative and afraid of taking risks.

WOMEN. More dressing to your age and less trying to dress away from it will be a good policy. More sophistication and less fussiness. Develop a better taste in colour contrasts.

AQUARIUS
January 21—February 19

DOMINANT FACIAL CHARACTERISTICS
Round or squarish face. Ruddy colour in men, women

need little make-up to look consistently healthy. Snub-nosed or squat nostrils impart a sense of fun to the face. Large eyes wear a permanent smile.

DOMINANT PHYSICAL CHARACTERISTICS

Stocky. Could be stout, even at a young age. Chunky, substantial type.

LOOK AFTER YOUR . . .

hair, which is likely to cause trouble early on. In men, it may recede quickly. In women, get thinned out and unmanageable if not very carefully attended to.

YOUR DRESS SENSE

Slightly old-fashioned, or 'square' might be a more contemporary term.

MEN. Try not to conform to type so much. For office wear —be more venturesome. For more free-and-easy occupations, sport more colour in shirts, ties, socks. Get away from the 'suit mentality' and experiment with 'separates'.

WOMEN. Reject the tweedy look for the more feminine. Be adventurous with colours and new materials. Inject more sex-appeal into your daily dress. For evenings out, reduce a stocky appearance with slimming patterns. Use your hairstyles to better advantage. There is something slightly motherly about your appearance. Offset this, if you want to, by adopting a more slinky look. You are quite capable of getting away with it.

PISCES
February 20—March 20

DOMINANT FACIAL CHARACTERISTICS

Intellectual-type features. Ascetic. Associated with artistic pursuits. Dark-eyed, high cheek bones. Hair predominantly dark, if not quite black. Women would have full red lips and men's mouths would be called sensual.

DOMINANT PHYSICAL CHARACTERISTICS

Well-built if not a bit on the slim side. Not, however, to be confused with thinness. Feet tend to be a little large. Hands, also, made for creative use, may be a bit bigger than normal.

LOOK AFTER YOUR . . .

complexion. Slight skin disorders may attack at any age. Keep away from too much sun-bathing as this could tend to dry up the skin and cause premature wrinkling. Women should be particularly careful as to choice of cosmetics. Men may find themselves allergic to certain shave lotions and hair preparations.

YOUR DRESS SENSE

Usually pretty well developed. You have to dress for various social events and are pretty well-versed in what to wear and when.

MEN. A little more taste may be necessary since there is a tendency to overdo things.

WOMEN. While being venturesome, don't overstep the mark in your search for individuality.

ARIES
March 21—April 20

DOMINANT FACIAL CHARACTERISTICS

Normally good looking. In women, handsome rather than pretty. Men tend to the feminine line while retaining masculine characteristics. Eyes, blue in more cases than none. Otherwise, green and hazel.

DOMINANT PHYSICAL CHARACTERISTICS

Powerful in men, well-built in women. Girls develop at an early age, men tend to spread before they should.

LOOK AFTER YOUR . . .

eyes, your weakest part. Regular visits to the optician are advisable. Avoid too much close work. Blue eyes are traditionally weaker than brown. If brown—there is little need for concern.

YOUR DRESS SENSE

Eccentric sometimes. An individualistic choice of colours, not always harmonious.

MEN. Tend to annoy their fellows with perverse ideas in masculine dress. They go too much to town in shirt colours, gaudy ties, shoes that are fashionable in a rather common way.

WOMEN. Use dress as a means of self expression and exhibitionism. Accentuate their sex in dress, prone to be risqué. Don't lose your sense of proportion in this. You are likely to be dubbed out of this world by your contemporaries if you do.

TAURUS
April 21—May 21

DOMINANT FACIAL CHARACTERISTICS

Large-faced. Flabby, perhaps, in later years, but that can be taken care of by restrained dieting. Brown eyes, rather small. Bushy brows, whether dark or fair. Hair with a receding line at an early age. In women, double chins will be the menace if dieting is not given extra thought. Pleasant faced people, the Taurians, nevertheless. Kindly and generally always smiling.

DOMINANT PHYSICAL CHARACTERISTICS

Portly, as the years roll by. Stout with women. Natural fat makes a comfortable looking body. Not unsightly, by any means. The sort of appearance that rouses feelings of domesticity, good mothering, a happy man with sporting instincts.

LOOK AFTER YOUR . . .

girth. Your biggest enemy. But it will naturally be well-developed. The secret will be to not let it get too much of a good thing.

YOUR DRESS SENSE

Difficult to plan, as sizes will present problems. Colours will be the predominating, saving grace.

MEN. Avoid loud checks, brilliant shirts, unconventional ties. But dress free and easy whenever time and place permits.

WOMEN. Wear pastel shades or dark colours. Never vivid contrasts. No horizontal stripes. Perpendicular stripes will flatter. Skirts not too tight. Hats will add to height if girth takes it away. Girlish ensembles will be out at a pretty early age, but youth can be maintained with a few good tips from those in the know. Small feet are likely to be another physical feature, so, for a good balance, wear flatties more often than not.

GEMINI
May 22—June 21

DOMINANT FACIAL CHARACTERISTICS

Thinnish, slightly strained-looking most of the time. An interesting face though, and one that commands attention. Thin nostrils show breeding. Eyes are deep set. A widow's peak more than likely in men. Very dark eyes, specially with women. Hair usually thick. Dry scalp will need care.

DOMINANT PHYSICAL CHARACTERISTICS

Tall. Men of six foot not unlikely. Women, shorter, but tall *for* women. Long arms. In women, particularly graceful legs and a well-defined figure. Men have a certain grace too.

LOOK AFTER YOUR . . .

throat and skin. Your throat is sensitive, though most ill-conditions will be psychological and easily curable with a little positive thinking. Any skin rashes must be carefully treated, but, again, these will be more easily traceable to the mind than to any deep-rooted physical condition.

YOUR DRESS SENSE

Well developed because dress is your main compensation for imagined troubles.

MEN. Will have quiet, well-bred taste but may be a bit afraid to break out in anything above the conventional smart attire.

WOMEN. Will tend towards sophistication in their choice of clothes. Separates will be worn more than anything else. Evening wear will strike many new notes. Quite daring separates will vie with ultra-smart suits and dresses. Hats will attract, with good heads to carry them. Shoes may present occasional problems.

CANCER
June 22—July 23

DOMINANT FACIAL CHARACTERISTICS

Changeable. Moody-looking at times. The next—the picture of happiness. Large eyes, sorrowful and joyful in turn. A generous crop of hair in men. Women love their tresses so much they have difficulty in parting with them for fashion's sake. High cheek-bones belong to the women. Men have their share also.

DOMINANT PHYSICAL CHARACTERISTICS

Delicate on first sight, really very strong on closer inspection. Wiry, the men run well and are rarely short of breath. Women whip around the house with plenty of energy in store. Gangling could well describe some men and gawky would sum up women. But a lot of attraction accrues from both states, for poise is obvious in all movements.

LOOK AFTER YOUR . . .

stomach, for gastritis can attack. Feeding habits, reformed, would help men and women over this stile.

YOUR DRESS SENSE

A rather careless attitude to dress is likely to spoil chances of looking really smart. Men are apt to look too casual.

MEN. Brush up on your club and town wear. Try to look less careless and devil-may-care at weekends. You can't quite carry it off.

WOMEN. Generally try to look younger than their years will allow. Cut down on the juvenile rigs and contemporary gear. Dress your age and you will get away with it every time.

LEO
July 24—August 23

DOMINANT FACIAL CHARACTERISTICS

Calm, placid features sometimes hide a restless spirit. Beetling brows overshadow eyes full of depth. Men have a tanned complexion whatever the weather. Women are apt to be highly coloured. Little make-up is necessary. Blue eyes are predominant in both sexes.

DOMINANT PHYSICAL CHARACTERISTICS

Average height and build. Deep chests mark the menfolk and ample bosoms delight the women. Middle-age spread is not likely to attack until past middle years—perhaps not at all.

LOOK AFTER YOUR . . .

chest, as bronchitis is likely to trouble you during winter months. Don't take vague chest pains too seriously. These will be, in the main, traceable to worry-thoughts and bouts of unnecessary anxiety. Keep as free as possible from coughs and colds.

YOUR DRESS SENSE

Misdirected ideas of chic may dismay when criticism comes along. You mean well, but need a bit of guidance now and again.

MEN. You are apt to mix your colours and fail to match them. Flamboyance strikes you as smart—but you have difficulty in carrying it off.

WOMEN. You also are venturesome, especially where colour-combinations are concerned. Hats fascinate you, but you do not wear them well. Study up on contemporary trends. Try to be more fashionable. Some of your ideas are a little trite and prosaic. Make the most of your dominant assets and then 'dress away' from them.

VIRGO
August 24—September 23

DOMINANT FACIAL CHARACTERISTICS

Red-heads are many under the Sign of Virgo. Also raven-haired beauties. Men have romantic faces. Women make the grade in films, or become the local femme fatale. Green eyes are many times seen. Pale skins add beauty to women. Men, too, are attractive in their way with a pallor women find irresistible.

DOMINANT PHYSICAL CHARACTERISTICS

Virile, active looking. Long bodies full of energy. Men are wiry, women elegant-limbed.

LOOK AFTER YOUR . . .

eyes, to prevent headaches. And your virility is under constant strain through trying to overdo things—mentally and physically.

YOUR DRESS SENSE

Surprisingly—for beauty in women and good-looks in men —dress sense falls by the wayside more often than not. This is largely due to too much concentration on face and too little on fashion.

MEN. You must remember that good looks are helped out by good clothes. Being pretty isn't enough. Brains are needed too—especially where dress is concerned. Do yourself proud by coming off the high horse and discarding those careless, casual clothes. Something in the city in the way of garb would sit well on you.

WOMEN. You, too, need to be less arty and high falutin'. Study that raven hair or those auburn locks, and dress accordingly. You can be classic—Grecian—even, and look extra well turned-out.

LIBRA
September 24—October 23

DOMINANT FACIAL CHARACTERISTICS

Fit looking. Clear skinned. Eyes sparkle most of the time.

Hair may not be too abundant after middle years in men. Muscles may get a bit too flabby too soon if exercises are not kept up. Women could go to seed prematurely if good care is not taken in the early twenties.

DOMINANT PHYSICAL CHARACTERISTICS

Smallish. Here and there and everywhere with great speed. Light on the feet, men, generally, are athletic and virile. Large hands can tackle delicate jobs surprisingly well. Women are agile too, built for active jobs.

LOOK AFTER YOUR . . .

kidneys and joints. Rheumatics may be your main trouble. Take extra care in winter months not to get damp—and stay damp.

YOUR DRESS SENSE

Well developed and cultivated. Most clothes worn sit well on men and women alike.

MEN. Go to town from time to time, for special occasions where your clothes are concerned. You can sport a few bright colours with aplomb.

WOMEN. For special occasions you could afford to experiment with unusual colours. You could carry off something quite revolutionary and be the envy of the neighbourhood. Don't wear headscarves or hats. Your head and hair do you great credit.

SCORPIO
October 24—November 22

DOMINANT FACIAL CHARACTERISTICS

Acquiline features. Prominent noses are no bad feature. Women have classic features in many instances. The menfolk have filmic faces. Deep eyes are always misleading the beholder.

DOMINANT PHYSICAL CHARACTERISTICS

Well-built men and women make Scorpions stand out in a crowd.

LOOK AFTER YOUR . . .

nerves. Your main trouble in life is an anxiety complex. This plays havoc with your stomach and is answerable for most of the conditions from which you suffer from time to time. Watch tendencies to lumbago in later life—too.

YOUR DRESS SENSE

Meticulous—you tend to overdo it at times. An innate sense of dress comes out from time to time. Generally, you can be trusted to wear the right thing at the right time.

MEN. Keep mainly to whites and pastel shades where shirts are concerned. Keep suits dark. Avoid hats if you can.

WOMEN. The same applies. In white, you look clean and antiseptic, which suits you well when you have to fight to get your own way. The sophisticated line is for you—to the point of severity. When you relax—don't go all to pieces in choice of clothes. Preserve that degree of cold chic men find most alarming—and disarming.

SAGITTARIUS
November 23—December 22

DOMINANT FACIAL CHARACTERISTICS

Not too strong looking but this is not necessarily true of your actual constitution of course. You might be described as 'delicate' looking.

DOMINANT PHYSICAL CHARACTERISTICS

Gangling, gawky, but an attractive frame that looks energetic, lithe and lively.

LOOK AFTER YOUR . . .

limbs. Rheumatics will be your main enemy. And nerves will tax you in times of stress. All curable by using the right diets, taking regular exercises daily and realising nothing is really as bad as it seems.

YOUR DRESS SENSE

Fussy, to hide inferiority in many cases. Try to make more of personality through the normal channels and don't rely on dress to see you through.

MEN. Less trimmings, such as tie-pins that are out-dated, glary ties and too bright socks.

WOMEN. Accessories can spell death to your best and smartest outfit. Don't overdo the earrings, beads, fancy handbags. Shoes must be chosen with extra care. Too much make-up is likely to spoil your delicate features and make a travesty of an otherwise attractive, appealing face.

CAREER INDICATIONS FOR THE TWELVE SUN SIGNS

CAPRICORN

M E N

Miners
Directors
Executives

Earthy occupations such as coal-mining, excavational work. Such men are found on archaeological expeditions. They search for uranium, precious metals and minerals from the bowels of the earth with whom they identify themselves. Or they are to be found creating, from bricks and mortar, from clay and crude iron—

buildings and edifices with which they link the upward trend of their ambitions. Capricornians are also at the heads of boards of directors. Are excellent executives. The word of command is for the man under the sign of Capricorn.

WOMEN

> Executives
> Career-girls
> Politics

Are ambitious. Career-girls develop into industrial leaders. They also become efficient executives—are the stuff from which female promoters of political movements are made. They stand for the rights of women in a masculine world, but do not lose their essential femininity in the process. These women are behind many a successful man whom they inspire with their courage and ambition. Trade union movements owe their drive to many women under Capricorn who make up for the less positive menfolk who come under their influences.

AQUARIUS

MEN

> Aviators
> Scientists
> Pioneers

Skyborn, they pioneer research into unknown elements of the Universe. Are behind many scientific researches. Gifted with probing minds, they contribute to progress in scientific fields. Nuclear weapons, electronic apparatus, radiological mechanics absorb the lives of these restless Aquarians. Even if only in small ways due to limited career-conditions, they see to it all life is a voyage of discovery.

WOMEN

Domestic
Science

The same may be said of women, who are likely to turn their enquiring minds to matters to do with progress in domestic science, and fields covering household gadgets for the ease and comfort of the housewife. Some stray from the home, to be lost forever in the world of science and forsake, for ever, the more romantic side of life.

PISCES

MEN

Seafaring men
Export - Import
Fishmongers

Find them on the high seas! In olden times, they were pirates, searching for hidden treasure. Today's Pisceans are never so happy than when on water. Sea captains, sailors, yachtsmen, boating enthusiasts are numbered among men under the sign of Pisces. And deep-sea divers in the tropics. And fishermen. Trawlermen in the oceans of the world owe their careers to Pisces. Higher up the industrial scale they are to be found in the export and import side of the fish business. Nearer to home, they invest in offshoots of their trade by owning or managing fish restaurants or fishmongers shops.

WOMEN

Designers
Leather workers

Show an interest in leather goods, industries connected with the boot and shoe trades. From workers in leather factories they can be designers of footwear, handbags, female leather accessories, finding, in these materials, everlasting sources of inspiration for their ever-present creative abilities.

ARIES

MEN

| Builders |
| Architects |
| Armaments |
| Steeplejacks |

Builders of buildings, architects of edifices. For ever looking upwards—Arians reach for the sky and find expression in construction. Or they span mental distances by physically building bridges —reach into the future by constructing roads. This typifies their never-ending search for perfection and the realisation of ambition and hope. Or the more restless Arian loves the noise of explosions, busies himself in an armament factory. Or becomes a good military man, living on an imaginary (or real) battlefield of noise and ballistic energy. If he is more subdued, he contents himself with dealing in arms, big and small. On the other side of the fence, he seeks excitement and reaches for the sky by being a steeplejack, climbing great heights for sheer joy and becoming one of industry's most essential craftsmen. Feet off the ground is the aim of the true Arian!

WOMEN

| Farming |
| Textiles |

Find them as lovers of animals, or, conversely, engaged in farming or in industries which turn fleece and wool into garments. On the other side, they can be engaged in fashion, in which materials such as wools and textiles largely feature.

TAURUS

MEN

> Stocks and
> Shares
> Livestock
> Tobacco
> Toys

Stocks and shares have a fatal fascination for some Taurean men. Mathematically-minded, they have an unerring aptitude for figures. They are found behind many a big deal and possess an almost feminine intuition for the right calculation at exactly the right time. In the West, find these men in charge of Ranches, commanding great herds of livestock. In other parts of the world, they are successful farmers and breeders. They are also fine horsemen or deal in horses both from an industrial and a racing angle. That little confectioner on the corner of the street, that tobacconist who stocks your favourite tobacco—is more likely than not to have been born under Taurus, for Taurians display great interest in such industries. Even toys for children have appeal for them. Many a happy child owes his joy to the inspiration of a Taurean man who has been visited with a particularly apt inspiration for a new-type toy for today's child.

WOMEN

> Saleswomen
> Design
> Executives

They also make good retailers in the sweets, tobacco and toy lines. Good saleswomen, with a mind for figures, they run many a successful business or are well-paid employees of chain-shop concerns. There is a metal with a peculiar fascination for them, and that is copper. Their menfolk are also interested in this, more, of course, from an investment angle. The Taurean woman, however, will use copper in a number of fascinating ways, as self-decoration or as a household appliance or fitting. A deep-down conviction that copper is *her* element drives her to be surrounded with it as much as possible.

GEMINI

MEN

Civil Service
Transport

Are Civil Servants—or, at least, betray signs of the 'civil service' mentality insomuch as they are precise in their business dealings and have a keen head for figures. Local authorities and municipal offices are their forté. Transport work appeals to them, both as drivers and executives. Railways and public transport concerns find a ready place for the Geminian mentality.

WOMEN

Civil Service

Are writers and journalists. Also they make good, efficient clerks. Civil service work is for them also. Cool-headed, they view life from a mathematical angle— are efficient managers in the home.

CANCER

MEN

Turn to interior décor for a profession if they can. Otherwise they fulfil this urge by being useful round the house, making it a thing of beauty for their womenfolk. Generally, the creative urge calls and they find expression in, perhaps, design

Décor.
Design
Engineering
Agricultural
work

for the theatre, screen or television. Soft furnishings and textile design are among other good outlets. The more practical are engaged in engineering projects, especially those connected with water—dams, viaducts, and so on. Agricultural work appeals, and many a fine farmer owes his love of the land to his Cancerian influence.

WOMEN

Domestic
service
Receptionists

Domestic service draws the Cancerian woman, though, in these days, in a smarter manner than in days gone by when domestic work was looked upon as an inferior occupation. Rather do they tend to turn towards work as receptionists, cooks to large, smart restaurants, housekeepers to well-off families. Among the lesser aspects of this work, chambermaids and waitresses feature largely. Domestic science attracts the more brainy Cancerian female, and not a few well-paid careers are carved out in this field.

LEO

MEN

Teaching
Commercial Art
Optical Trades

Teachers are made from men under Leo. They have a way with children and students. Their word of command holds attention, their minds are attuned to absorbing knowledge. They have great ability for passing this on to others. Art, also, in many forms, attracts the Leo man. He can be a success as a commercial artist, either in advertising, the theatre, film and TV world or as a straightforward portrait or landscape painter. But, in a commercially-minded world, he turns to advertising for most success and financial gain. Other forms of art attract him. Music, literature, dancing. The study of precious stones also holds fascination, and it is possible for him to become an expert in this field. He can also become a first-class specialist in the optical trades—either as an optician or on the development side of opthalmic manufacture.

WOMEN

Paper
Printing

The paper industry claims a great deal of Leo women. Pulping, preparation, processing and printing can be included. The Leo woman professes interest and ability in, and for, a great number of industries in which she is usually most successful.

VIRGO

MEN

Investigators
Police
Doctors
Osteopaths

'Private Eyes', policemen, detectives, investigators for insurance firms stem from a great number of Virgonians. Intuition, insight, a great knowledge of human psychology helps them to be both ruthless and understanding in dealings with those whom they have to investigate. They also make good doctors and back-room-boys in medical laboratories. They have a way with them of immediate appeal to those suffering from rheumatic disorders, and, in this, make excellent osteopaths and manipulators. They are in sympathy with the natural way of life and are likely to oppose orthodox medicine when commonsense dictates. The food industry owes a great deal to their foresight and discrimination and they can be, and are, responsible for many a drastic and necessary change of policy in a nation's feeding policy.

WOMEN

Make fine matrons in hospitals, or sympathetic nurses if they don't quite make the grade. They also have a hand in medicine, making good doctors and specialists. The natural way of life holds interest for them, and work of a missionary nature also attracts.

> Nurses
> Doctors
> Missionary
> Work

LIBRA

MEN

Social work is for the Libran. Welfare problems, under his surveillance, are easily solved. He has a sympathetic grasp of human nature. He is often a public figure and can rise to great heights in pursuit of the betterment of civilisation. On the more creative side—he makes an excellent specialist in the hairdressing trade and can understand and cater well for female likes and dislikes in this direction. Literature holds appeal, but he is more likely to attack the commercial side in favour of the art side in that publishing could be his forté more than an academic pursuit of good writing purely from an aestetic angle.

> Welfare Work
> Hairdressing
> Publishing

WOMEN

Floral work and horticulture claim many a Libran woman as she displays a particular aptitude for this kind of work. She

| Floral Work |
| Horticulture |
| Hairdressing |

is good at hair culture and many of her group have been, and can be, responsible for revolutions in hair care. She, also, is a literary type, but a taste for good books sometimes overcomes a business mind and she is more likely to pursue this vocation from an 'art for art's sake' point of view. She could write—were she to put her mind to it.

SCORPIO

MEN

| Naval Work |
| Surgeons |
| Chemical |
| industry |

On the high seas, they make good naval men. As marine workers, they contribute a great deal to this branch of science. Hospitals boast fine surgeons in the Scorpio group. This also includes dental surgeons. Commercial photography interests, and also chemical industries including food as well as pharmaceutical concerns. Many a good bar-tender is a Scorpio, and, higher up the social scale, a licensed victualler owes his success to this Sun Sign.

WOMEN

| Laundry |
| Soft Furnishings |
| Hospital |

Neatness and cleanliness in the home often urges a Scorpio woman to become connected with the laundering and soft-furnishing industries. Textiles and drugs have appeal, both from a design and production point of view. Sympathetic, industrious and successful midwives stem from this group and find fulfilment in private practice or in connection with hospital work. Essentially feminine— Scorpio women are thorough in all they do and work in these fields is always taken very seriously and dealt with diligently.

SAGITTARIUS

M E N

Banking
Insurance
Salesmanship
Publishing

Money-making is the dominant urge of the Sagittarian man. He invests skilfully. He is to be found as a bank clerk, better still, as a bank manager. He is a good insurance man, either as salesman or executive. The family man not engaged in these matters sees to it his family is well cared for financially and well-covered by insurance policies. The Sagittarian man always has his eye on the future—and his work is always carried on with this in view. He can also be engaged in ship building. General shipping interests play a large part in his life. Exporting and importing attract, in a variety of lines. He would make a good publisher and the world of ink would be lost were it not for many a Sagittarian.

W O M E N

Banking
Accountancy

Good business women, they find their way into the banking world, have a good brain for figures, can enter accountancy and be relied upon to run a business efficiently if so employed. Keenly interested in cash, they can both run a home successfully and attend to a career at the same time.

PRESENT AND FUTURE MOVES FOR MORE SUCCESS AT YOUR JOB

CAPRICORN

Try for more authority at your job. There is room for it if you approach a superior with tact. A few years from now could well see you earning twice your present salary.

AQUARIUS

Juniors at your place of work may be on the way to overtaking you. It is your job to make yourself indispensible. Try a few bright suggestions to those who are over you. There are certain aspects of your work presenting economic difficulties. These could be removed were you to use your initiative.

PISCES

Keep a tight hold on your present position. The future may well see changes, but these will be to your best advantage only when the time is ripe. Curb an impatient desire to be moving onwards. Your turn will undoubtedly come. Your present occupation is by no means the ultimate—there is plenty ahead.

ARIES

Considerable financial gains are likely in the foreseeable future. For now, however, be grateful for what you have. Superiors have their eyes on you and are marking your progress well.

TAURUS

If you are at sea with your present job, don't hesitate to get out while the goings good! You have many capabilities that are going to seed. Sound good friends for suggestions. Some time from now you will make good in a branch of activity at the moment unknown to you, but for which, nevertheless, you possess considerable potential.

GEMINI

Resist a rather 'strait-laced' attitude to your job. Be more adventurous! Your superiors are not quite so hard-headed as you think. There is a side to them you have not yet discovered. For the sake of future prospects—go out to find this. Quite probably they are waiting for you to approach them.

CANCER

If you have a desire to branch-out on your own, think well

before you take any drastic steps. You have a measure of security at the moment. If, however, the urge for individuality gets too great, plan ahead with care before taking the plunge. There are certain assets you possess that could make for a good individual career, but cash may be the one drawback in early days of a new venture.

LEO

Responsibility is the state you most desire at your job. Hang on for a bit longer. It will be on its way to you pretty soon! Meanwhile, make the most of that which your work has to offer. A course of night-school training in a particular facet of study that appeals might do the world of good in drawing the day of ultimate progress far nearer.

VIRGO

You may be a bit of a revolutionary. Trade union rules and convention may irk you. Have patience! Your day will come. Qualities of leadership you possess will not go unsung.

LIBRA

Your artistic outlook may annoy others. Try not to apply this to your job. Mechanical ways of thinking are more acceptable to your associates at work. Try to cater for their prosaic tastes if you want to work happily with them. Later, you will no doubt find ample chance to open up a branch of your work, at your present place of work, or somewhere else, in which your outlook will be given full expression.

SCORPIO

The future will probably hold many moves for you before you finally settle down. Accept these moves as all for your ultimate good—though they may seem a bit trying at the time. You are ear-marked for money—so try a little patience in the meantime!

SAGITTARIUS

If considering an outside job for a change—you may well be on the right road. But weigh well the cash hopes that might accrue from such a change. Stability is best in the long run, and you might be chasing an idle dream.

IN-A-NUTSHELL
BUREAU OF CAREERS FOR MEN AND WOMEN

Read these indications in company with the **CAREER INDICATIONS FOR THE TWELVE SUN SIGNS**—at the beginning of this Section

CAPRICORN
MEN. Builders, cement-mixers, bricklayers. Public or private concerns in capacity of director.

WOMEN. Private secretaries, shorthand typists, political and/or trade union executives.

AQUARIUS
MEN. Flyers, pilots, aircraft stewards, radio/TV mechanics. Nuclear scientists, radar, electrical engineering.

WOMEN. Air hostesses, dispensers, laboratory assistants.

PISCES
MEN. Fishermen (all branches of the fish trade). Employees in boot and shoe trades, or owners of own shoe shops, shoe repairers.

WOMEN. Leather goods designers.

ARIES
MEN. Architects, designers, draughtsmen. Builders, contractors, ballistic specialists. Steeplejacks.

WOMEN. Fashion experts, farmers, veterinary surgeons.

TAURUS
MEN. Farmers, breeders, tobacconists, financiers, accountants, clerks.

WOMEN. Saleswomen, interior specialists.

GEMINI
MEN. Civil servants, transport workers, drivers, bankers.

WOMEN. Writers, reporters, interviewers, clerks.

CANCER
MEN. Designers, engineers, agriculturists, dairy farmers, engineers.

WOMEN. Domestic service workers, housekeepers, receptionists.

LEO

MEN. Teachers, instructors, artists, designers, opticians.

WOMEN. Paper trades, printing, packaging.

VIRGO

MEN. Investigators, police officials, doctors, osteopaths.

WOMEN. Missionary and/or welfare workers, nurses, doctors.

LIBRA

MEN. Social workers, hairdressing specialists, publishers, writers.

WOMEN. Welfare workers, hairdressers, journalists.

SCORPIO

MEN. Sailors, sea-faring jobs in general, surgeons, pharmaceutical workers, victuallers, licensees.

WOMEN. Soft-furnishings, décor, hospital workers, laundry specialists.

SAGITTARIUS

MEN. Bankers, insurance brokers and/or salesmen, publishers, ship builders, shipping magnates.

WOMEN. Bank clerks, accountants, export and import clerks, stenographers, secretaries.

At the end of this book is a Section for parents—giving advice on probable careers for their children. Many parents hope their children will follow a chosen career, or take up where father left off, or follow in his footsteps.

This policy is, many times, fraught with disappointment. Parents fail to grasp that their child's inclinations may follow completely opposite directions and tastes. Furthermore, they do not take into consideration the all-important question of heredity. Son does not, of necessity, follow father, or daughter—mother. Generations hand on the ambition-spur and progress-drive, but do not necessarily hand it on from *father* to *son*. Facial and physical characteristics sometimes throw-back to the second and third generations. The same obtains with capabilities, abilities and 'gifts'.

Apart from this, there is the all-important question of the Star's influences upon children. Because the father was born in November—he naturally follows that which the November planet has to offer. His son, however, born in July, is bound to follow what July's planet has in store for him. How foolish is it then, to be annoyed and hurt when the son or daughter wants to go in the exact opposite direction to that which the fond parents hope?

Many successful family businesses and concerns have been created. Yours may be one of them. But there are cases (many) where the Stars will not be frustrated. To this, one must acquiese. Now—before we approach our children's future hopes, let us consider the material things contained in your Star Sign.

THE STARS TURN NOW TO THE MATERIAL THINGS CONTAINED IN YOUR STAR SIGN

Now learn the material things of your Star Sign. The metal or metals you should carry. The stone that will be your luckiest always to wear as a ring, a brooch, a locket, a necklace or in the form of earrings.

And consider your colours, which should always be worn in your dress, even if only as a scarf, a handkerchief, or any sort of accessory. Your colours could be carried in your handbag or in your wallet.

See if the number of your house or flat contains your special number. Or if an Insurance Policy number contains it, or a membership number. Your number possesses great significance. Be sure it is on your person in some shape or form. Make your most important appointments on days in which your number falls.

Pin-point your best day of the week for accomplishing things that most matter to you and pay particular attention to your choice of friend or marriage partner according to the indications you will read in this section.

Where friends and relations are concerned, consider *their* metals, stones, colours when buying them gifts. Remember their best days and their significant numbers and base all you do with and for them on those portents.

By now you should have massed a wealth of knowledge with which to control and plan your future moves. You should also be extra popular with your friends and family, for you hold in your head and your hands a complete guide to *their* future hopes in life.

Pass on this vital knowledge. Trace the progress and future hopes of your children by the signs and indications contained in this book. Where your important business and career-moves are concerned—get to know all you can, (through this book) of the significant characteristics of those upon whom you depend for future happiness and success.

Now make a close study of what remains to be told. . . .

PART FIVE

Your Star Sign

Showing your Metal, Stone, Colours, Numbers, Herb, Days, future finances and who best to mix with or marry.

CAPRICORN
December 23—January 20

SATURN
Ruling Planet

INDIVIDUAL METAL. Lead.

SYMPATHETIC STONE. Turquoise, Moonstone or Garnet.

HARMONIOUS COLOURS. Brown and Grey.

TO PROTECT YOU FROM . . . Selfish people, being afraid.

SYMPATHETIC HERB. The Yew.

LUCKY NUMBER. 8. The Ambitious Number.

LUCKY DAY. Saturday.

HEALTH AND YOUR NUMBER. Health improves as you grow older.

FUTURE FINANCES THROUGH NUMBER 8. Being practical will help you make money and keep it.

MIX WITH OR MARRY . . . CANCER, Number 2. Your best chances of future marital happiness lie with a partner born under Cancer. Friends, also, should be chosen from this group if you wish for fullest co-operation in all your financial problems and career-hopes.

AQUARIUS
January 21—February 19

SATURN
Ruling Planet

INDIVIDUAL METAL. Lead.

SYMPATHETIC STONE. Garnet, Moonstone or Amethyst.

HARMONIOUS COLOURS. Pink, Blue, Nile.

TO PROTECT YOU FROM . . . Jealousy. To give you Spirituality.

SYMPATHETIC HERB. The Yew.

LUCKY NUMBER. 4. The Resourceful Number.

LUCKY DAY. Sunday.

HEALTH AND YOUR NUMBER. Physical strength, powers of endurance. But excesses would prove harmful.

FUTURE FINANCES THROUGH NUMBER 4. Working extra hard most of the time will be the best way of making money.

MIX WITH OR MARRY . . . VENUS, Number 6, or LIBRA, Number 6. Two choices here for success in life where marriage is concerned. You have a choice of friends, too, with whom to enjoy life, socially and from a business point of view.

PISCES
February 20—March 20

JUPITER
Ruling Planet

INDIVIDUAL METAL. Tin.

SYMPATHETIC STONE. Amethyst, Aquamarine or Bloodstone.

HARMONIOUS COLOURS. White, Pink, Green.

TO PROTECT YOU FROM . . . Deceitful People and Jealousy.

SYMPATHETIC HERB. The Thistle.

LUCKY NUMBER. 7. The Number of those who are Outspoken.

LUCKY DAY. Monday.

HEALTH AND YOUR NUMBER. Strong, wiry, but mind-strain might bring on unnecessary complications.

FUTURE FINANCES THROUGH NUMBER 7. A great variety of jobs and many outlets, creative and constructive, would lead to much cash.

MIX WITH OR MARRY . . . JUPITER, Number 3. A sympathetic, kind partner will be found in a Jupiter mate, someone with whom you could share your troubles and triumphs. Friends, too, under Jupiter, would be ready to give you a helping hand, especially if you are a social climber.

ARIES
March 21—April 20

MARS
Ruling Planet

INDIVIDUAL METAL. Iron.

SYMPATHETIC STONE. Bloodstone or Aquamarine.

HARMONIOUS COLOURS. Pink and White, Red and Cream.

TO PROTECT YOU FROM . . . Anger. Self-gratification. Depression.

SYMPATHETIC HERB. Wormseed.

LUCKY NUMBER. 9. The Optimistic Number.

LUCKY DAY. Tuesday.

HEALTH AND YOUR NUMBER. Blood-stream and circulation to be cared for. Otherwise strong. Don't get morbid.

FUTURE FINANCES THROUGH NUMBER 9. Holding a position of trust will be the key to your financial successes.

MIX WITH OR MARRY . . . LEO, Number 1. A positive personality is what you seek in marriage, and a Leo subject will be more than positive. In your search for friends, you will look for the *individual* rather than for the conservative type. A Leo will vie with you in individuality and be willing to break the bonds of convention when required.

TAURUS
April 21—May 21

VENUS
Ruling Planet

INDIVIDUAL METAL. Copper.

SYMPATHETIC STONE. Lapis Lazuli or Rock Crystal.

HARMONIOUS COLOURS. Red and Yellow.

TO PROTECT YOU FROM . . . Angry Associates. Feelings of Complacency and Pride.

SYMPATHETIC HERB. The Yarrow.

LUCKY NUMBER. 6. The Artistic Number.

LUCKY DAY. Friday.

HEALTH AND YOUR NUMBER. Good health. Kidneys to be watched, though. Eyes also.

FUTURE FINANCES THROUGH NUMBER 6. Cash will come to you with little effort.

MIX WITH OR MARRY . . . AQUARIUS, Number 4. A fiery, rebellious partner with a will to win will be best for you. Someone willing to share ups and downs. One who recognises the artistic side of life, and who does not sacrifice principles for easy ways out. Friends in the Aquarian set will be of the same mind as you—productive, creative, eager to give something to the world.

GEMINI
May 22—June 21

MERCURY
Ruling Planet

INDIVIDUAL METAL. Silver.

SYMPATHETIC STONE. Agate or Emerald.

HARMONIOUS COLOURS. Red, Blue and White.

TO PROTECT YOU FROM . . . Smugness, Self Opinionation, Opposition. To show you the lighter side of life.

SYMPATHETIC HERB. Valerian.

LUCKY NUMBER. 5. The Tolerant Number.

LUCKY DAY. Wednesday.

HEALTH AND YOUR NUMBER. Always feed your good appetite. But guard against getting impurities into your blood-stream.

FUTURE FINANCES THROUGH NUMBER 5. Luck, chance and good fortune will, in the main, be the determining factors where your cash is concerned.

MIX WITH OR MARRY . . . VIRGO, Number 5. Like will mix with like. Harmony will be found with a Virgo subject. Tastes will be similar and it will be a case of perfect agreement on almost everything. Friends, also, will be fast and genuine.

CANCER
June 22—July 23

MOON
Ruling Planet

INDIVIDUAL METAL. Silver.

SYMPATHETIC STONE. Emerald or Agate or Pearl.

HARMONIOUS COLOURS. Green and Brown.

TO PROTECT YOU FROM . . . Misleading Factors, Envious people. To prevent your being Selfish.

SYMPATHETIC HERB. Wintergreen.

LUCKY NUMBER. 2. The Perceptive Number.

LUCKY DAY. Monday.

HEALTH AND YOUR NUMBER. You may be a sluggish type. Care of your digestive organs is advised.

FUTURE FINANCES THROUGH NUMBER .2. Thrift will get you what you want. Save for the future, that's your best bet.

MIX WITH OR MARRY . . . CAPRICORN, Number 8. For a partner who will be good to you in your old age. And for someone who will allow you freedom of action to pursue your great ambitions. Friends under Capricorn will listen to your ideas, heed what you say and take action to help you.

LEO
July 24—August 23

SUN
Ruling Planet

INDIVIDUAL METAL. Gold.

SYMPATHETIC STONE. Onyx or Ruby.

HARMONIOUS COLOURS. Red and Green.

TO PROTECT YOU FROM . . . Making Hasty Decisions. From the Wrath of Others. From Powers that might seek to Usurp you.

SYMPATHETIC HERB. Wake Robin.

LUCKY NUMBER. 1. The Intellectual Number.

LUCKY DAY. Sunday.

HEALTH AND YOUR NUMBER. Excellent health. Could be marred only by excessive worry over small matters.

FUTURE FINANCES THROUGH NUMBER 1. Your pile will be made through many ways, most of them fairly easy. You should not want for much, eventually.

MIX WITH OR MARRY ... SCORPIO, Number 9 or **ARIES,** Number 9. Fighting partners, these. You would have your disagreements and fights, but their wills to win would spur you on to fresh efforts. And having the last word would be a constant, invigorating challenge. Friends in the Scorpio and Aries groups would make life continually exciting.

VIRGO　　　　　　　　　　　　　MERCURY
August 24—September 23　　　　　Ruling Planet

INDIVIDUAL METAL. Silver.

SYMPATHETIC STONE. Cornelian, Moonstone or Sardonyx.

HARMONIOUS COLOURS. Gold, Blue and Black.

TO PROTECT YOU FROM ... Hatred. Malice. To help you to see the Finer Things of Life.

SYMPATHETIC HERB. Valerian.

LUCKY NUMBER. 5. The Tolerant Number.

LUCKY DAY. Wednesday.

HEALTH AND YOUR NUMBER. Eat wisely. Dieting will be good for you.

FUTURE FINANCES THROUGH NUMBER 5. Clever calculating and a wise eye on current cash trends should make your financial future fairly sound.

MIX WITH OR MARRY . . . MERCURY, Number 5. Another case of similars doing well together. No 'yes' man attitudes will prevail. Absolute mental, physical and spiritual harmony could be achieved. A happy coterie of friends should be established, all Mercurians.

LIBRA
September 24—October 23

VENUS
Ruling Planet

INDIVIDUAL METAL. Copper.

SYMPATHETIC STONE. Peridot, Chrysolite or Sapphire.

HARMONIOUS COLOURS. Black, Crimson and Light Blue.

TO PROTECT YOU FROM . . . Opposition. To bring you Affection, Popularity, and a sense of the higher, more Spiritual things in life.

SYMPATHETIC HERB. Yarrow.

LUCKY NUMBER. 6. The Artistic Number.

LUCKY DAY. Friday.

HEALTH AND YOUR NUMBER. Good. Eyes will need looking after. Ease up on 'tension' thoughts.

FUTURE FINANCES THROUGH NUMBER 6. Clever calculations and strokes of luck will help you make good money. Little manual work, plenty of brain work could make you fairly well off.

MIX WITH OR MARRY . . . AQUARIUS, Number 4. A spirit of adventure in an Aquarian partner would appeal to you. Friends could make life great fun if from this group. Your partner would carry you along on a tide of daring and dashing speculation, both materially and emotionally.

SCORPIO
October 24—November 22

MARS
Ruling Planet

INDIVIDUAL METAL. Iron.

SYMPATHETIC STONE. Aquamarine, Beryl or Opal.

HARMONIOUS COLOURS. Brown and Black.

TO PROTECT YOU FROM . . . Grasping people. Moodiness and Depression.

SYMPATHETIC HERB. Wormseed.

LUCKY NUMBER. 9. The Optimistic Number.

LUCKY DAY. Tuesday.

HEALTH AND YOUR NUMBER. Strong, Virile. Over-doing things likely to be your greatest enemy against sustained health.

FUTURE FINANCES THROUGH NUMBER 9. Responsible positions will be yours if you wish to be in on the big time where cash is concerned. You will have to give good value for great trust that could be placed in your money-making capacity.

MIX WITH OR MARRY ... Leo, Number 1. A partner with whom to lead an exciting life will be found in the Leo group. Companions of the same group will be exhilarating and more than good for you in career and social life.

SAGITTARIUS
November 23—December 22

JUPITER
Ruling Planet

INDIVIDUAL METAL. Tin.

SYMPATHETIC STONE. Topaz.

HARMONIOUS COLOURS. Gold, Red and Green.

TO PROTECT YOU FROM ... Evil Seekers after your Possessions. Those who try to Dominate you.

SYMPATHETIC HERB. The Thistle.

LUCKY NUMBER. 3. The Sensitive Number.

LUCKY DAY. Thursday.

HEALTH AND YOUR NUMBER. Good powers of recovery from most ailments.

FUTURE FINANCES THROUGH NUMBER 3. The fairly easy way for you where cash is concerned. Money will beget money. Investment and speculation could be your strong points.

MIX WITH OR MARRY ... PISCES, Number 7. Children of such a union should be healthy, intelligent. A partner under Pisces would be a mystic—gifted with unusual powers. Friends under Pisces would further your ambitions for you by being able to see things otherwise hidden from you.

Here is a specimen Astrological Summary-Sheet. Reproduce this on separate sheets of paper and work out the Astrological characteristics and portents for you, your friends and family.

NAME ....

Date of Birth .... Sun Sign .... Ruling Planet ....

Number of House and Sign of Zodiac ....

Main Weak Characteristics ....

Main Strong Characteristics ....

Dominant Ambitions ....

Chief Capabilities ....

PSYCHO-TYPE ....

Constitution .... Vitamin Needs ....

Deficiency Mineral ....

Facial Characteristics ....

Physical Characteristics ....

Metal .... Stone .... Colours ....

Herb .... Lucky Number .... Lucky Day ...... Month ......

Meet or Marry .... (Star Sign and Number)
Here show general matter—Phobia, Peak Age of Power, Diet, Breathing Exercises, Peak Age of Virility, Sense of Humour, Main features of Love Life, Dress Sense, Future Financial Hopes, Investments to Make, Career to choose or improve Hopes, Investments to Make, Career to choose and improve upon. (General Summary of all matter not itemised in detail above, but in remaining sections of this Guide)

Signed .... Date ....

SUMMING-UP

The Stars pass into Orbit and leave you to your Future Hopes

The meaning of Astrology. The Star's Influences on the time you were born. Your Positive Planning Months. Your Month to Marry. Parents' Guide to their Children's Marriage Hopes. Parents' Guide to their Children's Career-Hopes.

THE STARS PASS INTO ORBIT AND LEAVE YOU TO YOUR FUTURE HOPES

Are you surprised that so many things in life can be influenced by the Stars?

Perhaps you are now asking yourself what place Providence has in this vast scheme? Well, Providence put the Stars in the heavens in the very first place, to guide the wanderer by night. But the Stars were also meant to guide the wanderer by day—in fact—throughout his whole life.

So keep your faith in Providence—or to whatever Power you resign your life and destiny. All is one great Circle of Life—one great Plan to keep the whole world turning in the vast Universe. And *you* are an important part of it. Your past, present and future really *matter*. Make the most of the knowledge you now possess. Pass it on to your friends and family and help them on *their* way.

Don't allow yourself to confuse Astrology with Psychology, (study of the mind), Graphology, (Character through handwriting), Astronomy, (study of the heavenly bodies, their positions, movements and magnitudes), Phrenology, (study of bumps), Palmistry, (fortune-telling from the palms of the hands).

Be clear as to the *true meaning* of Astrology.

It is the study of predestination by the Stars gauged through and by the influence they exert on the world and the individual.

There are ten planets which include the Sun and the Moon. Strictly speaking, the Sun is a star but is listed as a planet.

Your horoscope is a plan of the heavens as they are at the time when you were born. A true horoscope is a detailed analysis of such a map, and it is from this map your life's course is predicted. From this you are told the weakness and strong-points in your character make-up.

In this book, general indications have been shown, from which you are able to identify your own and those of your friends and relatives.

There is no doubt whatsoever that the Stars (planets) *do* exert good and bad influences upon individuals. This is borne out in thousands of cases of great, sometimes identical, similarity between two or more people born under the same Sun Sign.

A Scorpio is easily recognisable because he has to fight all the way. His planet is Mars, the god of war and conflict. This is just one example. That is why two Scorpios, for instance, would make bad marriage partners. Think of both of them fighting, all of the way, and together! And for life!

Perhaps you would like to know what particular influences the Stars have over people according to the approximate time they were *born*?

You were born at dawn . . . You are the restless type.
You were born just after dawn . . . You might be rich.
You were born before noon . . . You could be lucky.
You were born before bedtime . . . You will have fun.

When you are having your horoscope cast—it is always very important you give your correct time of birth. There is a variation for almost every hour of birth from dawn to dusk—from midnight to midnight.

Born at dawn . . . Life is just beginning, you are restless to get going, to begin to live, to make your way in life.

Born after dawn . . . Life has begun, opportunities are presenting themselves to you. All is now in motion.

Born before noon . . . Night has passed, fiction of dreams has vanished. Fact now takes over and the law of luck is in action.

Born before bedtime . . . Day is done, the evening's pleasures lie before you. Work accomplished, you take your reward for hard effort.

Throughout each year, you have ups and downs. Some months seem more favourable than others.

Sometimes you say 'What a pity I did not decide to see So-and-So last month instead of this'. 'We should have booked our holiday for next month instead of for early September'. 'I feel sure that if we draw out that Policy next July instead of June—we will get far better value from any investments we make'.

Here are the Positive Planning Months for each Sun Sign. Use them to get the best out of your future plans for each year. And advise your friends and relations—when they are planning *their* monthly moves—

Your Sun-Sign	Your Positive Planning Months	Choose this Month to marry
Capricorn	— May. September	... May
Aquarius	— June. October	... June
Pisces	— July. November	... November
Aries	— August. December	... August
Taurus	— January. September	... September
Gemini	— February. October	... February
Cancer	— March. November	... November
Leo	— April. December	... April
Virgo	— May. June.	... May
Libra	— February. June	... June
Scorpio	— March. July	... March
Sagittarius	— April. August	... April

PARENTS' GUIDE TO THEIR CHILDREN'S MARRIAGE HOPES

The Capricorn Girl will have many affairs before settling down.

The Aquarian Girl will make a good, moneyed marriage.

The Piscean Girl will have a hard task catching her partner.

The Arian Girl may marry into high circles.

The Taurean Girl will make a business-partnership union.

The Gemini Girl will be gay. Marriage may well be late in life.

The Cancerian Girl will have an adventurous love life.

The Leo Girl will undertake great responsibilities in marriage.

The Virgo Girl may be a career-girl, and marry into her job.

The Libran Girl will have lots of children, marry well.

The Scorpio Girl will make a tempestuous marriage, full of fun.

The Sagittarian Girl will be sporty, marry into society.

The Capricorn Boy will shun marriage until career is finalised.

The Aquarian Boy will marry more than once.

The Piscean Boy may well marry someone older than himself.

The Arian Boy will marry beneath him, but make a great job of it.

The Taurean Boy will be a flirt, will marry late in life.

The Gemini Boy may marry a partner who will improve his social status.

The Cancerian Boy will have a long search for a suitable partner.

The Leo Boy will marry young.

The Virgo Boy may have a childless, but happy marriage.

The Libran Boy will put career before marriage, but will love well.

The Scorpio Boy will make an intellectual marriage.

The Sagittarian Boy may marry into country stock.

PARENTS' GUIDE TO THEIR CHILDREN'S FUTURE CAREER-HOPES

CAPRICORN BOY. Practical. Thrifty. Scholarly. Good to equip him for a definite trade. Building, construction work, etc. He could hold a supervisory position. Not exactly a gamesman—so make him use his brains. Will have a head for figures when fully mature.

CAPRICORN GIRL. Precise. Houseproud. A good wife later but would take kindly to a career early on. Design. Secretarial Work. Will have a tendency to put over strong feelings of conviction on a certain chosen subject. Leader type. Train her to be top-dog, at least over her feminine friends. If she shows a desire to be ordinary—let her alone. But watch for signs of *individuality*. She might be worth a *good* education and grounding in a woman's profession.

AQUARIUS BOY. Hard worker—even at play. Intense in all he does. Play fair with him. Try not to deny him anything that would help him further his thirst for knowledge. Back-room-boy type. Head buried in books. Don't check this. Or he may swing to the opposite and seek adventure and thrills in speed and heights. Anxious moments could come—but give him rope. He'll look after himself and probably end up being something quite big. Invest cash in his future. It will be well repaid.

AQUARIUS GIRL. Also bookish, serious. Capable of great insight. Don't expect great things during schooldays but afterwards—she will break out and reach for the sky. Be tolerant. Career-girl type—she will need all your support in whatever vocation she picks. It will probably be something rather masculine. But don't fear. Underneath—she will be a true female.

PISCES BOY. Could run away to sea. Don't stop him. He has adventure in his blood. And guts. Consider also, a good, sound trade in case he does not display an adventurous spirit after all. He will be keen on footwear. Leather goods. Strange—but these will hold fascination for him. Many a useful, moneyed career has been forged in that trade.

PISCES GIRL. Neat, orderly mind. Handy with the needle. Inventive. Creative. Encourage her to express herself in artistic endeavours. Continue this after her normal schooling is over. She could do you credit.

ARIES BOY. Give him pencil and paper. But don't expect pretty drawings. This boy could design buildings. Or factories. Or churches. He will show a fascination for heights. He will have no fear of them. Do not check this. He will be perfectly safe. It's in his blood. On the other hand, if the Armed Forces call him, let him go without regrets. He won't be a ranker for long. Nuclear warfare will interest him from a scientific point of view. Or he may study explosives from a commercial viewpoint. Make enquiries before he has advanced much into his 'teens. This way, you will be ready to help him forward as much as possible. Place him in the Army if he wants—or investigate Government schemes for assisting a boy in ballistics.

ARIES GIRL. At an early age she will show great compassion for animals. Buy her a domestic pet. Later, she could well enter the humane activities—become a vet, a farmer. Conversely, if she grows smart and sophisticated, don't be surprised if she wants to make clothes, design hats or dresses. Something to do with fashion, anyway. Until she is in her middle 'teens, she will be rather undecided. But don't despair! She is the sort to see the light—in a flash. Then she will be well on her way—provided you do your best to help her and don't get the fixed idea you want her just to get married and settle down—soon!

TAURUS BOY. Rather likely to welcome cash with open arms in later life. And it will come to him fairly easily too. Don't try to keep too much of a parental eye on him. He is the stuff of which farmers or financiers are made. See him, eventually, as a director of a big firm, or owner of a thriving business he has built up himself. Consider, if you can, laying-by some cash for his late 'teens or early twenties to invest in something really sound and stable for his future. He may need a bit of help in early days. But, once on his own—there will be little to stop him forging ahead.

TAURUS GIRL. If your daughter talks a lot, don't mind! She will be persuasive—full of personality. That means she will make a good business woman. Sounds a bit stiff and starchy. But there have to *be* good businesswomen —and the Taurus girls go that way very often. She *may* not get beyond the sales floor of a retail house, but, on the other hand—she could end up by being a Buyer for a firm of some repute.

GEMINI BOY. Found, later in life, in a bank, or a post office. Or—higher up the scale, in Government offices. What will it be for *your* Gemini boy? It depends a great deal on what you do for his education. What standards you set him —at home, at school and in the years after he has left school and starts out in real earnest. He will chase good luck. Be on the wings of a prayer for many years before he takes root. But when he does settle down—it will be for keeps in a good position. Look at the other side of the picture. He may not, after all, be the civil servant, government official type. He may be too much of a mixer—a boy with the lads. In that case, he will love speed and movement. The industry that sets wheels in motion—takes people from here to there. That means transport—in some shape or form. Buy him a car— if you can afford one. Don't fear accidents. He will keep his two feet on the ground.

GEMINI GIRL. She may have a nose for news. In which case, the daily press may attract her. Or she could be one of those girls who write sensational first-novels when barely out of their school uniforms. Encourage her literary tastes. Read all she writes—if she shows you any of it! Or, if she has winning ways and a pretty face—she may want to spend her time meeting people and helping them. A receptionist, for instance, would be an ideal occupation if she shows sociable tendencies. At all costs, encourage her to be an extrovert —to meet people. To do things. To go places. To try new, exciting experiences. She won't let you down. Will probably make you very proud of her!

CANCER BOY. A saver. Stop him from getting a bit mean, though. Teach him how to *give*. He will have a strong engineering turn of mind. After school, encourage evening classes—or—better still, a continuation school where he can develop his abilities. He may, though, show a strong liking for agricultural work, so do not be surprised if he dislikes town life, yearns for the wide open spaces.

CANCER GIRL. Home-loving, she may want—later in life—to look after people, apart from a husband and children. See she studies domestic science. Or a larger perspective might embrace hotel work, information bureaus, receptionist's work. She could even manage her own hotel—in the long run.

LEO BOY. Will not want for much. Will want to teach. Or lead others. Or form groups. Or be head of movements agitating for this and that. Help him to make lots of friends. And, if one of the professions such as Opthalmy interests him, let him have his head. Government grants can be arranged. Otherwise, put yourself out to save a bit to give him a real good chance. He could make a fine optician, or be connected, in a useful and a lucrative way—with the opthalmic sciences.

LEO GIRL. Don't be surprised if she likes books, paper, pens, pencils. Give them all to her at an early age. Later, read her school reports with care. You will probably find she is interested in words, grammar, the English language. She will be likely to display an interest in types, in print, book design, magazine make-up. Her feminine touch could be brought to bear on the printed word, printed promotion, art and print work in the daily press world. In commercial art.

VIRGO BOY. A cool customer when it comes to figures! A few headaches perhaps, because he will want to bury his head in a book on mathematics, algebra or logarithms rather than go out for a long, healthy walk. But it will bode well for his future. Because this calculating mind of his will show he wants to be—or could be—a useful member of either the medical, nature cure or police professions. His searchings for the perfect, the deliberate calculation, the precise, the *definite*, all point to his desire to be a perfectionist. In this —you must help him. However trying it may seem in the early years.

VIRGO GIRL. A good bedside manner will make her well-loved. Later, a hospital would be glad of her services. A doctor would welcome her. She, also, will be a perfectionist. Spotlessly clean in habits. Precise.

LIBRA BOY. Flamboyant, slightly exhibitionist, he will be full of high ideals that he will want to force on the world. And he will find his outlet in literature. In writing. He could be a first-class journalist. Or novelist. Or serious writer. In all cases—he will be very successful. He will be keen on welfare work. As a long-distance shot, and, failing all these things, do not be surprised to find him developing an interest in the ways females look! In this, he could be a hair specialist. And a good one, too!

LIBRA GIRL. Also a literary type, keen to mix, to record sights and sounds. A good imagination should be developed to the full. Also, the Libra girl would make a tip-top hair culturist. Or manage a milliners. Or design hats!

SCORPIO BOY. Good capacity for making money, mainly in a supervisory position later in life. A fighter, he will battle every shilling of his way through life—and make pounds in the long run. The licenseeing trades will have appeal. May be a bit tee-total, but will see cash in the game. Or expect him to excel in chemistry at school. This may well have a great influence on his future career. He will have experimentation in his blood. Again, don't be surprised if he betrays an interest in doctoring. He may be a bit forthright—but you will soon be able to detect the makings of a bedside manner in him! Again, he may wander down to the docks a lot, or to the seashore, or show interest in ships. Don't stifle this urge. He may be looking for his sea legs.

SCORPIO GIRL. Comfort, and the love of it, may make her thoughts wander to the house beautiful. And then she will be well on the way to what may be a career in soft furnishings, textile designing and/or interior décor. Or she may be overcome with sympathy for mankind and decide to go in for some branch of hospital work. If she is exceptionally brainy, and you have helped her as much as possible— she may even make a doctor.

SAGITTARIUS BOY. Big-money ideas will occupy the thoughts of the young Sagittarian—and, when teenage is reached—he will want to start doing something about it. A school of accountancy would not be a bad idea if he shows tendencies to be quick on the uptake with figures. Otherwise —the open road and salesmanship may call. This could mean big money also, for the Devil would order the Bible from him without demur. He may fancy ship-building, so, if he plays with toy boats in his bath—let him!

SAGITTARIUS GIRL. Found in banks, and that's where she may be in later years. Or possibly she may end up, before she marries, as a private secretary to a very smart man in a very smart firm. Why not? Big business will have an attraction for her. Or she will be someone's right-hand-man, slick with the filing cabinet and keeping some office in good order. Don't think she will be de-glamourised. She will have to keep up appearances to hold down a good job.

NOW LOOK TO THE FUTURE

That is your story in the stars—and the story of your family and your friends. Now look to the future, and help those near and dear to you to plan for their future as well.

When things are going well for you, and your friends are on the up-and-up, and members of your family have triumphs, successes and victories, you can thank your lucky stars—and tell them to do the same!